A Living Hope

A Living Hope

A COMMENTARY ON 1 AND 2 PETER

ROBERT H. MOUNCE

Wipf & Stock
PUBLISHERS
Eugene, Oregon

Wipf and Stock Publishers
199 W 8th Ave, Suite 3
Eugene, OR 97401

A Living Hope
A Commentary on 1 and 2 Peter
By Mounce, Robert H.
Copyright©1982 by Mounce, Robert H.
ISBN: 1-59752-074-8
Publication date 1/27/2005
Previously published by Wm. B. Eerdmans Publishing Co., 1982

CONTENTS

A COMMENTARY ON 1 PETER

A COMMENTARY ON 2 PETER

TRANSLATIONS CITED

ASV   *American Standard Version*
AV   *Authorized Version*
Berkeley   *The Berkeley Version of the New Testament*
Goodspeed   *The New Testament: An American Translation*
Knox   *The New Testament in the Translation of Monsignor Ronald Knox*
LB   *The Living Bible*
Moffatt   *The New Testament: A New Translation*
Montgomery   *The Centenary Translation: The New Testament in Modern English*
NASB   *The New American Standard Bible: New Testament*
NEB   *The New English Bible: New Testament*
NIV   *The New International Version*
Norlie   *The New Testament: A New Translation*
NTBE   *The New Testament in Basic English*
Phillips   *The New Testament in Modern English*
Rotherham   *The Emphasized New Testament: A New Translation*
RSV   *The Revised Standard Version*
TCNT   *The Twentieth Century New Testament*
Weymouth   *The New Testament in Modern Speech*
Williams   *The New Testament: A Translation in the Language of the People*

A COMMENTARY ON
ON
1 Peter

INTRODUCTION

The letter we are studying claims to have been written by "Peter, an apostle of Jesus Christ" (1:1). For many this straightforward affirmation settles the question. Since the author identifies himself as the apostle Peter, we should look no further—unless, of course, unexplainable difficulties arise as a result.

And difficulties there are for some. For example, the Greek of the epistle is polished, has a number of syntactical subtleties, and shows evidence of a literary acquaintance with the Septuagint. Is this not too much to expect from an untrained Galilean fisherman? Secondly, the author's many references to the persecution of Christians betrays a later historical period when the Christian faith was a serious breach of public law, not merely a social annoyance. This would place the time of composition well after the death of Peter—probably during the tumultuous days of Domitian or Trajan. Furthermore, the author is thought to have depended upon the writings of Paul for much of his material (e.g., 1 Pet. 2:13-17 may be based on Rom. 13:1-7). For one of the Twelve who never enjoyed a close relationship to Paul this would be too much to accept. Finally, there are simply too few references to the teaching of Jesus to have been written by one of Jesus' own disciples.

Detailed answers to these objections can be found in the extended discussions of New Testament Introductions (e.g., Guthrie, Harrison). For the moment it is enough to remember that the so-called "literary" problem may be explained by the ancient custom of giving considerable freedom to a secretary (note 5:12, "With the help of Silas ... I have written"); the "persecution" of the letter, even 4:12ff., can be explained better in the context of the reproach in which believers were held than in a massive empire-wide program to eliminate Christians; similarity to Paul's teaching is actually congruence resulting from a common catechism that permeated the early church; and to argue against authorship on one's contemporary view of what should have been written is a methodological fault of serious proportions.

The case for Petrine authorship is as strong as one could expect from a writing as ancient as 1 Peter. Alternate suggestions (a pseudonymous letter, an anonymous letter attributed to Peter) are not persuasive.

The letter was written to "God's elect ... scattered throughout Pontus, Galatia," etc. (1:1b). Consequently, some have thought that the readers were Jewish-Christian believers. Sections such as 4:3-4 (which speaks of their having lived like pagans in "debauchery, lust, drunkenness, orgies, carousing and detestable idolatry") suggest much more strongly a predominantly Gentile-Christian audience. There is little doubt but that the congregations scattered throughout Asia Minor were in the main groups of believers who had rather recently come to faith in Christ (see 2:2, 10).

And where was Peter when he wrote to the churches? According to 5:13 he appears to have been writing from "Babylon." Calvin, intent on undermining Roman Catholic claims regarding Peter and Rome, said the letter originated in Mesopotamian Babylon. Few, if any, have accepted this hypothesis. Apparently there was a military outpost on the Nile that was also named Babylon. Could this have been the point of origin? No reason exists, however, that would lead us to locate Babylon in Egypt. The rather obvious answer is that "Babylon" is a cryptic and symbolic way of referring to the city of Rome. The practice is repeated often in the book of Revelation (e.g., 14:8; 17:5). The most probable date for the writing of 1 Peter is shortly before the persecution by Nero in AD 64.

One question remains, and that has to do with the nature and purpose of the work. One prominent interpretation is that in some way the letter had its origin in the rite of baptism. Preisker saw 1:3–4:11 as a baptismal homily. Cross held that in 1 Peter we have the Celebrant's part of an Easter baptismal service. While the baptismal motif is certainly present in the letter (note, however, that the word *baptism* occurs only at 3:21), the letter deals primarily with suffering and persecution. It is best to take 1 Peter as a genuine letter (circular, in that it was to be read to a number of churches) written to encourage believers in Asia Minor to expect and endure the hardships that were bound to come as a result of their commitment to the Christian faith.

①

FIRST PETER ONE

FROM PETER TO CHRISTIAN PILGRIMS (1:1-2)

1 *Peter, an apostle of Jesus Christ.* What a sense of wonder must have laid hold of Peter the former fisherman when he first grasped the full import of all that had taken place in his life since leaving his nets to follow Christ. It began that day when his brother Andrew made the startling announcement, "We have found the Messiah." Peter was brought to Jesus, who said to him, "You are Simon, the son of John. You will be called Cephas," which in Greek is *Petros* (Peter), a stone (John 1:42).

In ancient days names were intended to describe what the person would be like. Sometimes they were changed at critical points in a person's life. For example, Jacob, the supplanter (one who takes the place of another, especially by trickery; see Gen. 25:19-34), became Israel (he who strives with God) after the long night of wrestling with the angel on the bank of the Jabbok (Gen. 32:22-29). Simon's change of name didn't immediately alter his character. When he cowered before the accusations of a maiden at the gate of the high priest's courtyard (John 18:17), he was by no means "rocklike." But God was not through with him yet. Christian character is not forged overnight. Becoming all that we were meant to be requires a long and laborious process. You've probably seen the lapel button that says, "Please be patient: God has not finished with me yet."

This same Peter who so often during his years of apprenticeship had allowed enthusiasm to control his actions (for example, it was Peter who underestimated the faith required to walk on water; Matt. 24:28-31) was now a seasoned apostle of Jesus Christ. He had been commissioned by the risen Lord and sent out to proclaim the message of God's love and salvation. As an apostle he had been given the authority to speak and act on God's behalf.

Peter addresses his letter to *God's elect*. The idea of a chosen or elect people comes from the Old Testament. In Deuteronomy 14:2 Moses told the tribes of Israel, "The Lord has chosen you to be a people for his own possession." The prophet Isaiah repeatedly referred to Israel as chosen by God (Isa. 41:8; 44:1; 45:4). But now Peter transfers this concept to the Christian community. We are God's elect. The church is one with Israel in its special relation to God. In the parable of the vineyard (Matt. 21:33-43) Jesus teaches that Israel's inheritance is taken and given to others. In killing the son the tenants incurred the wrath of the owner of the vineyard and lost all claim to the kingdom of God. That the church is now the Israel of God (Gal. 6:16) is one of the great foundational truths of New Testament theology.

While it is a great honor to be among the elect, we must remember that God's purpose in election is to set apart a people to fulfill *his* purposes. Election involves responsibility and accountability. The Lord told Ananias that Paul was his "chosen instrument to carry [his] name before the Gentiles and their kings and before the people of Israel" (Acts 9:15). Later in 1 Peter we will learn that Christians are chosen so that they may "declare the praises" of God (2:9). Election serves the purposes of God, not the pleasure of those who are chosen.

Peter also addresses his readers as *strangers in the world*. The Greek word is instructive. It is found twice in the Greek version of the Old Testament. When Sarah died in the land of Canaan, Abraham went to the Hittites and said, "I am a stranger and a *sojourner* among you" (Gen. 23:4). The Psalmist confesses the transitory nature of man's life upon the earth with the words, "I am thy passing guest, a *sojourner*, like all my fathers" (Ps. 39:12). The word emphasizes that one's true citizenship is elsewhere. The sojourner passes through this life as a visitor from another world who has no intention of settling down away from home. We sing, "This world is not my home, I'm just a passing through." Perhaps Hebrews 11:9-10 provides the best commentary available: Abraham "made his home in the promised land like a stranger in a foreign country, . . . for he was looking forward to the city . . . whose architect and builder is God."

This picture of the believer with his true citizenship in heaven while temporarily away from home on earth is strengthened by the accompanying phrase, *scattered throughout Pontus, Galatia,* etc. The word *diaspora* (Dispersion) was a technical term for Jews in exile living outside of Palestine. Applied to the church it emphasizes that we are a heavenly people (Phil. 3:20) who for the moment are passing through a foreign land. The *RSV* translates "exiles of the Dispersion." Geographically the provinces listed lie mostly in the central and northern parts of Asia Minor.

2 This verse consists of three distinct phrases that expand the idea of election. The *NIV* supplies *who have been chosen* to bring out the connection with verse 1. It is worthy of note that all three persons of the triune God are included in the three descriptive phrases. Each has a specific role in the electing process.

First of all, believers have been chosen *according to the foreknowledge of God the Father.* Election is based squarely on the wisdom and knowledge of God. It is fruitless at this point to quibble about whether or not God elects on the basis of knowing ahead of time what man will choose to do. What we do know is that although God's decrees are absolutely sovereign, they do not in any way override the freedom of man to decide.

The purpose of election is *obedience to Jesus Christ.* We have been chosen to obey. Freed from sin by our union with Christ, we are now to live a life of obedience to him. In Romans 6 Paul compares two slaveries—one to sin that leads to death and the other to obedience that leads to righteousness (Rom. 6:16). To be freed from sin is to become a slave of righteousness (Rom. 6:18). To have been elected by God means to have entered into a life of obedience to Christ. There is no other alternative.

Exactly what *sprinkling by his blood* means is not clear. The *TCNT* translates "to be purified by the sprinkling of the Blood of Jesus Christ," apparently with the idea that when we fail to obey we need the continuing cleansing of Christ's death for sin (see 1 John 1:7). Kelly says that, stripped of metaphor, it connotes "accepting His saving death by faith and entering the new community inaugurated by it" (*A Commentary on the Epistles of Peter and Jude*, p. 44).

If the basis for election is the foreknowledge of God and its purpose is obedience to Christ, the means by which it is carried out is the *sanctifying work of the Spirit.* God's Spirit is actively engaged in setting people apart (that is what "sanctify" means) to a totally different kind of life. He awakens our hearts to respond to God and his goodness. He draws us away from the allurements of a sinful world and enables us to follow the path of holiness. He is the great Sanctifier. To set the mind on the Spirit is life and peace (Rom. 8:5-6).

One writer points out that the entire first chapter of 1 Peter is an expansion of three terms: foreknowledge (3-11), sanctification (13-17), and obedience and sprinkling (18-25). In fact, the entire letter is a commentary on them (Bigg, *St. Peter and St. Jude*, p. 95).

Grace (God's favor toward men) may be a Christian variation of the normal secular word of greeting (*charis* rather than *chairein*). *Peace* is the Hebrew *shalom* with its emphasis on well-being. Peter prays that these divine favors may be bestowed *in abundance* upon all believers in Asia Minor to whom he writes.

BORN ANEW TO A LIVING HOPE (1:3-12)

3 Peter opens the first major section of his letter by ascribing praise to *the God and Father of our Lord Jesus Christ.* This designation is heavy with theological significance. In the Old Testament God was praised as the One who created the world and redeemed the children of Israel from Egyptian bondage (Pss. 104–106). Now he is praised because as the Father of Jesus Christ he has provided by means of the resurrection a new birth into a living hope. God is not remote and unknowable. He has revealed himself perfectly in the person of his Son. Paul declares in Colossians 1:15 that Christ is "the image of the invisible God." The One who cannot be seen has become visible in his Son. As the author of Hebrews puts it, God has in these last days spoken to us, not through an occasional prophetic voice or vision but by his own Son (Heb. 1:1-2). Although no one has seen God, he can now be known since the "Son, who is at the Father's side, has made him known" (John 1:18).

The full name of the Son is the *Lord Jesus Christ*. Jesus is his given name. Joseph was instructed by an angel to call him Jesus "because he will save his people from their sins" (Matt. 1:21). But he is also Lord. This title (*kyrios*) was regularly used in the Greek Old Testament to translate the Hebrew for God. To call Jesus Lord is to declare that he is God. Jesus is also Christ (or Messiah). He was anointed by God (*Christos* means "the anointed one") to carry out his redemptive plan in history.

God is further described as the One who *has given us new birth*. He has "caused us to be born again"—that is what the verb (which occurs only here and in 1:23) means. The remarkable change that takes place when a person comes to faith in Christ demands vivid imagery. The idea of "new birth" boggled the mind of Nicodemus (John 3:3-9). It still puzzles those who would like to understand it apart from personal participation in the experience.

This new birth is based on God's *great mercy*. God saw us in our need and was moved with compassion. Ephesians 1:4 reminds us that God is "rich in mercy." Not only was Jesus filled with tenderness when he saw the hungry crowd, but he also provided them with all the bread and fish they could eat (Matt. 15:32).

Peter continues by noting that our new birth is *into a*

living hope. This hope, which the author of Hebrews calls "an anchor for the soul" (Heb. 6:19), is living because it is based in the *resurrection of Jesus Christ from the dead.* Because he lives, we too shall live. Apart from the actual bodily resurrection of Jesus we would have no valid basis for believing in existence beyond death. Because Jesus has returned from the other side of the grave, we have a living hope. As Paul triumphantly declares, "Where, O death, is your victory? Where, O death, is your sting?" (1 Cor. 15:55).

4 Not only are we born again into a living hope, but *into an inheritance* as well (the phrases are parallel). Unlike earthly inheritances, which are apt to *perish, spoil or fade,* this inheritance is preserved *in heaven* for the believing church. The land of Canaan was the inheritance of the Old Testament people of God. The Israelites were told that they would be richly blessed "in the land the Lord your God is giving you to possess as your inheritance" (Deut. 15:4; note that the Greek Old Testament uses the same word that occurs in the text of 1 Peter). The inheritance of the New Testament Christian, however, is infinitely more than Mideastern real estate. It is full and final deliverance from the curse of sin and all its debilitating effects. It is that state of perfect holiness which follows the final removal of sin and Satan (Rev. 20:10, 14). As such it is "a perfect inheritance beyond the reach of change and decay" (Phillips).

5 Not only is the inheritance being kept in heaven, but faithful believers are living out their lives here on earth *shielded* (or guarded) *by God's power.* God has not left the church without protection in the midst of a hostile world. He continuously guards (the verb has military connotations; see 2 Cor. 11:32) his own. We can be absolutely confident that God will see us through until the day we receive our inheritance. Yet it is *through faith* that we are kept. Faith is not to be thought of as some meritorious work that serves as a basis for awarding eternal life. Yet it cannot be ruled out as the appropriate human response to God's offer of love and mercy. Without faith God's keeping power would be theoretical only.

God's people are guarded until *the coming of the salvation that is ready to be revealed in the last time.* This salvation is the final eschatological deliverance from all the persecution and sorrow that will result from Satan's final assault. Revelation 12 tells of Satan being cast out of heaven and filled with fury "because he knows that his time is short" (Rev. 12:12). The *last time* is not the period of final judgment but the time of persecution and trouble that precedes the return of Christ. When he returns, the church will experience the great deliverance.

6 Peter goes on to say, *In this you greatly rejoice.* There are three basic words in New Testament Greek that express human joy. One has to do with the benefits of health and happiness, another with the subjective feeling of joy, and the third with the outward demonstration of joy and exultation (*New International Dictionary of New Testament Theology,* II, 352). Peter uses the third term. He calls for outward rejoicing (the verb may be imperative rather than indicative) in view of everything that has just been mentioned (a living hope, an imperishable inheritance, the protection of God, and eschatological salvation).

The call to rejoice is not qualified by the fact that for a time believers may have to suffer all sorts of trials. Joy amid tears is a Christian phenomenon. In the context of Peter's letter *all kinds of trials* refers not to inner struggles with sinful appetites but with trials that come from without. To be shielded by the power of God does not mean to escape the opposition of a hostile world.

7 God has a reason for sending trials. *These have come so that your faith . . . may be proved genuine.* Peter stresses the appropriateness of having one's faith tested. He calls attention to the fact that gold, although of less value, is nevertheless *refined by fire.* If gold, which perishes, is subjected to fire in order to burn away the dross, how much more important is it to faith that all counterfeit and alien elements be removed by trial. The "testing of your faith" refers not to the experience of trial but to that which proves to be genuine as a result of trial. This is that which is so infinitely more valuable than gold. One cannot help but recall the counsel of James, "Consider it pure joy, my brothers, whenever you face trials of many kinds" (Jas. 1:2).

Genuine faith will result in *praise, glory and honor* when Christ returns. On that day men will by the faith they have sustained bring praise and honor to God. They will not have trusted him in vain. Every knee shall bow and every tongue confess the greatness of his redemptive love (Phil. 2:10-11). At the same time the faithful will receive their "well done, good and faithful servant!" (Matt. 25:21). They will share in the glory and honor of that great and festive day when *Jesus Christ is revealed.* In this context the revelation of Christ does not mean the arrival of someone who has been absent but the unveiling or disclosure of the One who has been spiritually present all the time. The truth of the matter is that Jesus is not spatially separated from his church. Did he not say, "Surely I will be with you always, to the very end of the age" (Matt. 28:20)? His "coming" is simply his visible disclosure. This revelation takes place at the end of time (v. 5) when the faithful receive their eternal reward.

8 When Peter writes *though you have not seen him,* he is contrasting his experience as a disciple of Jesus with that of his readers who had no occasion to encounter Jesus during the time of his earthly ministry. They are able to "see" Jesus only with the eye of faith. Yet they *love him* (the Greek word is the celebrated *agapaō* that so often in Scripture is used of God's love for man; see John 3:16). The context suggests a deep sense of personal affection for the One whom they have never met in person but whose presence in a spiritual sense is beyond question.

The contrast in the second clause of verse 8 (*even though you do not see him now*) is between the believers' present situation and what will happen at the return of Christ. The word *now* has the idea of "yet." In the preceding verse Peter had spoken of the day when Christ would be revealed. So even though his readers had not yet seen Christ in his triumphal return, they nevertheless continued to *believe in him.* In spite of "grief in all kinds of trials" (v. 6) they remain steadfast in their commitment to the One whom they as yet have not seen except through the eyes of faith. It is because they believe that they are *filled with an inexpressible and glorious joy.* It is "inexpressible" because language itself is inadequate to communicate fully the experience of knowing Christ. It is "glorious" because it stems from the One to whom all glory belongs (see John 1:14; Rev. 5:12).

Some have asked how Peter can speak of joy in the midst of suffering. Is that not an impossible contradiction? By no means. Suffering can be, as it *is* for those whose faith remains firm, a purifying experience. As fire removes the dross when gold is refined, so suffering removes the impurities that keep the believer from that intimacy of personal relationship which always results in joy. The promise of inexpressible and glorious joy is realized by every Christian who maintains his faith in times of severe testing.

9 The *goal* or outcome *of [their] faith* is *the salvation of [their] souls.* This statement is primarily eschatological. When "Jesus Christ is revealed" (v. 7) and we see him (implied in v. 8b), we will then receive the reward of faith—the salvation of our souls. Peter uses the word *soul* for the entire nature of man. In the words of another disciple, John, "When he appears, we shall be like him, for we shall see him as he is" (1 John 3:2). The beatific vision will transform the believer. At that moment we will be like him. This is what "salvation" or deliverance really means—freedom from sin with its power to distort and destroy the human soul.

The present participle translated *for you are receiving* (v. 9) suggests that this salvation, however, is something more than eschatological deliverance. It is going on right now. Believers are even now in the process of being saved (see 1 Cor. 1:18). We are filled with joy precisely because even at the present time we are receiving that deliverance which, when Christ returns, will be made complete. That which belongs to the end of time is now being realized by those who have by faith already entered into eternal life.

10a Having mentioned salvation as the goal or outcome of faith, Peter lingers for a moment on the subject in order to show how New Testament salvation is related to Old Testament prophecy. The prophets who spoke of this bestowal of God's favor (*the grace that was to come to* believers) "pondered and explored" the theme (*NEB*). The word translated *searched intently* is used in Hebrews 11:6 of that active and earnest seeking after God apart from which no one can come to him. To enter God's presence we must first "believe that he exists" and second "that he rewards those who earnestly seek him."

10b, 11   The prophets searched *with the greatest care.* The picture that emerges is of prophets examining with care and precision the content of their own prophecies. They searched for clues that would suggest the *time and circumstances* connected with the advent of the Redeemer who would suffer and then be glorified. To the Jewish mind the concept of a suffering Messiah was unacceptable. It involved an essential contradiction. In spite of passages such as Psalm 22 and Isaiah 52:13–53:12 the idea was rejected. That the Messiah should be glorified was entirely appropriate. Psalm 2 taught that he would rule the ends of the earth with an iron scepter, while Psalm 110 said that he would crush the rulers of the whole earth. But popular Jewish sentiment found inadmissible the divine order that suffering must precede glorification. The prophets knew it but were unable to understand when and under what circumstances this would all take place.

It is worth noting that it was the *Spirit of Christ* in the prophets who predicted these sufferings and the subsequent glories. The "Spirit of Christ" is the "Holy Spirit" of verse 12. He was decidedly active in the old dispensation (see Gen. 1:2; Num. 24:2; Judg. 14:6; etc.). His association with divine utterance is clearly established in 2 Peter 1:20-21, which indicates that prophecy is the result of personal reflection by men who were "carried along by the Holy Spirit."

12   To the prophets *it was revealed* that in predicting the sufferings of Christ *they were not serving themselves* but a later generation of believers. Their careful study of all the evidence was not in itself adequate to the task. Insight must be *revealed*. Technical exegesis of Scripture may prepare the way for understanding, but in the final analysis it is the Spirit of God who reveals the real meaning and significance of biblical truth. While the prophets did not learn the exact "time and circumstances" when their message would be fulfilled, they did understand in a general way that it belonged to a later generation.

The account of the sufferings of Christ and the glories that follow forms the content of *the gospel*. The "good news" (and that is what "gospel" means) is that because Christ has suffered for the sins of man he is entitled to the glory that follows (see Phil. 2:6-11). The path to eternal joy leads through the deep valley of sorrow. When man accepts by faith the promise of God, he is delivered from the guilt and power of sin. This is "good news" for those who yearn for something better than slavery to sin! This good news has been brought by *those who have preached the gospel to you.* A human instrument has been used. At the same time, however, it can be said to have been proclaimed *by the Holy Spirit sent from heaven.* While the message can be recited by man, it reaches the inner recesses of the human heart only as a result of the convicting power of the Holy Spirit. He is the One who "will prove the world wrong about sin and righteousness and judgment" (John 16:8). He comes "from heaven" in fulfillment of Jesus' promise that when he went back to the Father he would send the Counselor to them (John 16:24, 28). Thus we see that the Holy Spirit bears a threefold relationship to the gospel: he was active in its Old Testament formation, in its New Testament proclamation, and (by extension) in its contemporary application.

Peter adds that *even angels long to look into these things.* While there is no Greek word in the text translated "even," the idea is appropriate to the context. The gospel is so important that even heavenly beings want to "bend down and take a look." While the verb may indicate nothing more than an inquisitive glance, here it means "to pore over or to study intently."

A SERIOUS CHALLENGE TO HOLY LIVING (1:13-25)

13 Someone noted that when you see a *therefore* you should check to see what it is there for. In this case Peter is about to state the ethical implications that follow logically from the doctrinal teaching of the preceding paragraph. Because believers have received a salvation sufficiently great to give rise to inexpressible joy in the midst of suffering, a new and different kind of life is expected.

The first requirement is, *prepare your minds for action.* This translation (*NIV*) misses the vividness of the imagery. In the ancient Eastern world men wore long robes, tied around the waist with a belt or girdle. When strenuous action was called for, they would tuck the long folds of the robe under the belt to provide maximum freedom of movement. To "gird up the loins of your mind" (*AV*) means to bring under control all loose-flowing thoughts that would impede spiritual progress.

The second requirement is similar: they are to be *self-controlled.* The Greek word means "to be sober." Without balance and full control men are liable to reel back and forth between various intoxicating ideas about doctrine and conduct. The proper response to the grace of God is disciplined self-control.

Finally, they are to *set [their] hope fully on the grace* that is theirs. Most commentators understand this as a gracious act of divine favor given when Christ returns. On the basis of what happened when Christ came the first time, put your full confidence in what will take place when he comes again. Others call attention to the present participle in the phrase "the grace that *is being brought* to you" and interpret the exhortation to mean that believers are to trust without reserve in the grace of God that is now being revealed day by day. There exists a progressive revelation of God's grace to all who live in fellowship with him. Neither interpretation rules out the other. It is both/and, not either/or.

14 There is an important shade of difference between the translation *obedient children* and the literal rendering of the Greek, "children of obedience." The exhortation in verse 14 is not that God's children be obedient but that they conduct themselves as those in whom the spirit of obedience dwells. Their response to the gospel is twofold. Negatively, they will no longer conform to their evil desires (v. 14); positively, they will live lives of holiness (v. 15). The *ignorance* in which they formerly lived was characteristic of the first-century pagan world. While acknowledging that gods existed, people believed that they were either unknowable or unconcerned about man. Men allowed their lives to be shaped and molded by their own *evil desires*—by "the passions which once swayed you in the days of your ignorance" (*TCNT*).

15 Rather than conforming to evil desires, children of obedience will want to *be holy.* To be a child of God it is necessary to bear a family resemblance. God is by nature holy. The basic meaning of the Greek word is "different" or "separated." God is totally separate from sin. "Holy, holy, holy is the Lord Almighty," intoned the seraphs in Isaiah's vision (Isa. 6:3). Since God is holy, his children are to be holy *in all [they] do* (the word translated "conversation" in older versions means "conduct," "behavior," "way of life"). Sanctification is a theological term describing the ethical change that takes place in the life of the believer. It involves deliverance from the domination of evil and transformation into the likeness of God.

16 Holiness is required because *it is written* in the books of Moses, *Be holy, because I am holy* (see Lev. 11:44, 45; 19:2; 20:7). The fundamental basis for holy living is the same in the New Testament as it was in the Old. The conduct of believers in every age is determined by the nature of God. A holy God requires holiness in his followers.

17 Jesus taught his disciples to pray, "Our Father in heaven" (Matt. 6:9). Peter now cautions his readers not to presume upon this relationship. God is *a Father who judges each man's work impartially* (compare Peter's words in Acts 10:34). A holy God requires holiness in his people. In this context "work" refers to the demand for holiness in one's daily walk. The intimacy existing between Father and Son heightens the obligation for a changed life. (For the teaching of judgment based on works see also Rom. 2:6; Rev. 20:13.) The Greek may be translated, "If you call on him as Father." This expresses the intent of the passage.

Since we call upon God as Father for help (as the middle voice of the verb suggests) and know that he shows no favoritism, but judges all men by their action, we should *live [our] lives as strangers here in reverent fear*. The Christian lives out his days on earth as one whose permanent abode is elsewhere. His citizenship is in heaven (Phil. 3:20); he is only a sojourner here below. This sentiment is clearly expressed by an inscription ascribed to Jesus and found on the gateway to a large mosque in India, "The world is merely a bridge; ye are to pass over it and not build your dwellings upon it."

To fear God is not to cower before a capricious potentate but to stand with reverential awe in the presence of the creator and redeemer of mankind. He is the One who bought us back from slavery, not with silver or gold but by the sacrificial death of his Son. The historical background for this imagery is the Old Testament Exodus (Exod. 6:6-7). As God by his acts of mighty power brought the Israelites out of physical bondage in Egypt, so by the death and resurrection of his Son he leads his children out of spiritual slavery.

18 In Mark 10:45 Jesus declares that he came "to give his life a ransom for many." It is the verb form of "ransom" that Peter uses. Jesus *redeemed* us: that is, he paid the ransom. In ancient times it was possible for a slave to save up his earnings and in time, if conditions were just right, to purchase his freedom. The reference to *silver or gold* suggests that this was the idea in Peter's mind. But silver and gold can never buy the spiritual freedom men need. They have no value whatsoever in reference to man's need to be freed from the *empty way of life handed down* from those who have gone before. The ancient world lived largely without hope. If the future is without meaning, the present is futile—motion without progress, vain, pointless, and empty.

19 But Jesus paid the price. He *was* the price. He gave himself as the ultimate sacrifice for man. He offered himself to God as a *lamb without blemish or defect*. The terms refer to the ritual requirements of Old Testament sacrifice (Exod. 12:5; Lev. 22:19-21). Jesus by his death becomes the sacrificial Lamb of God. John the Baptist announced the advent of Jesus' public ministry with the words, "Look, the Lamb of God, who takes away the sin of the world!" (John 1:29). Paul declared, "Christ, our Passover lamb, has been sacrificed" (1 Cor. 5:7). When we grasp what it cost God to free us from sin, we will respond with reverential awe and renewed commitment to live a holy life.

20 That Christ would be offered as a sacrificial Lamb was determined *before the creation of the world*. Calvary was not an alternate course of action that had to be followed when some prior plan ran amuck. Not only the coming of the Messiah but his death on the cross as well were established in the councils of eternity. But now *in these last times*, that is, in this final epoch of world history which began with the coming of Christ (see Heb. 1:2; 9:26), he has been revealed *for [our] sake*. It was for us that Jesus came to earth, lived out his days, died, and rose again. It was for us that the price was paid. Considering the cost, one wonders how it could be that rebellious man should be so highly esteemed by God. Amazing grace!

21 It is through Christ that we are able to *believe in God*. Early in the life of the Jerusalem church Peter had boldly declared before the ruling elders of Judaism, "There is no other name under heaven given to men by which we must be saved" (Acts 4:12). He is the true and living way (John 14:6). That he was not merely human was proven by the fact that God *raised him from the dead*. This great event is the keystone of the Christian faith. Someone is said to have asked Tolstoy, the Russian novelist, how to start a new religion. His answer, "Have yourself crucified and rise again the third day."

God also *glorified* his Son. He exalted him to the highest status and gave him a name above every name. In due time all shall bow before him and confess his universal sovereignty (Phil. 2:9-11). All of this is so that our *faith and hope might be in God*. God ordained our salvation and through the obedience of his Son made it a reality.

22 Those to whom Peter writes are said to have *purified [themselves] by obeying the truth*. Obedience to that which a person knows to be right inevitably purifies the moral consciousness. Doing the right thing leaves a clean feeling. It is one of the fringe benefits of a righteous life. In context, however, the "truth" is undoubtedly the gospel message. By submitting to its demands those who believe are purified, that is, forgiven. The Greek perfect participle ("purified") refers to a decisive act in the past, the consequences of which continue in the present (compare *gegraptai*, "it is written," as used in reference to Scripture).

One result of inner cleansing is *sincere love for [one's] brothers*. The *TCNT* translates, "So that there is growing up among you a genuinely brotherly affection" (a rather lengthy but accurate paraphrase of the three Greek words). The mutual affection shared by natural brothers is, in this larger setting, extended to the entire family of believers. Christians love one another because they are brothers and sisters in a great spiritual family. God is our father and Jesus Christ is our elder brother (see Heb. 2:11, 17). For this very reason we are to *love one another deeply, with all [our] hearts*. "Intensely and heartily" is Goodspeed's translation.

23 To enter the family of God requires a new birth (see John 3:3). Those to whom Peter writes have been *born again*. They have been born into the realm of the spiritual. Unlike natural birth that results from *perishable seed*, spiritual birth is by the *living and enduring word of God*. Note the contrast between the seed that is perishable and the word of God that is living and enduring. Natural life results from physical birth and is temporary. But spiritual life results from the word of God and endures forever. Since the word is "living" it can create life, and since it "endures" that life is sustained for eternity.

24, 25a Peter quotes from Isaiah 40:6-8 to emphasize

the enduring quality of the word of God. Grass withers and flowers drop off (and men are like grass), but *the word of the Lord stands forever*. Jesus had taught that not the smallest letter or the least stroke of a pen would disappear from the Law until everything would be accomplished (Matt. 5:18). Man's life is a mist that appears and then vanishes (Jas. 4:14). God's word, however, is eternal. In a day of constant change man needs some source of stability, something that endures. Only God and his word provide such permanency.

25b The chapter ends with Peter reminding his readers that the message *preached* to them was the eternal and changeless word of God. It is "good news" because it alone remains unchanged by time. The Christians to whom Peter was writing had heard the message, responded to its radical challenge, and entered a life of obedience and brotherly love.

②

FIRST PETER TWO

THE LIVING STONE AND THE NEW ISRAEL (2:1-10)

1 New birth issues in new life. Believers have been "born again" by means of the "word of God" (1:23) and must of necessity reflect in the way they live this radical transformation. So Peter writes, *Therefore, rid yourselves of all malice.* "Malice" is a broad term for all sorts of evil and wickedness. The four nouns that follow specify more closely what malice covers in this context. Note that the four vices are the very ones that would be especially destructive of brotherly love (see 1:22).

Deceit is a major weapon in the arsenal of those who would manipulate others for personal advantage. *Hypocrisy* means acting a part. It describes those who pretend to be something they are not. *Jealousy* inevitably rears its ugly head in every setting where concern for one's own status is greater than concern for the welfare of others. *Slander* is backbiting, gossip, defamation of character. The Christian is to put away, or strip off (see Eph. 4:22, 25), everything that makes it more difficult for brotherly love to flourish.

2 Instead of malice the believer is to crave the "sincere milk of the word" (*AV*). The *NIV* adopts an interpretation of *logikos* that makes the phrase read *pure spiritual milk.* In Stoicism the *logos* was the principle of divine reason. It pervaded the universe. Hence anything that was *logikos* would relate to this divine *logos* and therefore be "spiritual." But Peter has just written about the word (*logos*) of God (1:23),

and this is what he has in mind as he counsels his readers
to long for its spiritual nourishment as a newborn babe longs
for his or her mother's milk. In terms of his longing for spiritual nourishment the Christian is always a "newborn babe."

The purpose of such nourishment is that by it we may
grow up unto *salvation*. Christian maturity brings deliverance. Growth is evidence of progress in the Christian life. It
is the word of God that feeds the soul, bringing health and
spiritual strength. Deprive a Christian of the word of God
and his life will shrivel and dry up like an unwatered plant.
Perhaps the greatest need in contemporary Christianity is a
renewed appreciation of the role of Scripture in the personal
and spiritual growth of believers. Jesus told his disciples,
"Apart from me you can do nothing" (John 15:5). For us this
means, Apart from God's word we can do nothing.

3   This verse connects loosely with what precedes. The
idea, however, is that we are to long for the sincere milk of
the word *now that* (or since) *[we] have tasted* (and found)
that the Lord is good. The expression comes from Psalm 34:8,
"Taste and see that the Lord is good." To have tasted the
goodness of the Lord is to create an enormous appetite for
all he has to offer.

In verses 4-10 we learn the true nature and function of
the church. Throughout this section Peter draws heavily upon
the Old Testament to describe the true Israel of God.

4   The first image we encounter is the *living Stone.* It
(or he) is "living" in that, having been raised from the dead,
"he cannot die again" (Rom. 6:9). He is "a life-giving spirit"
(1 Cor. 15:45). This Stone has been *rejected by men but chosen by God.* In the parable of the vineyard (Mark 12:1-11)
Jesus quoted Psalm 118:22 ("The stone the builders rejected
has become the capstone") to indicate that although he would
be rejected by men he would, in the purpose of God, become
the capstone of the kingdom. The destiny of ancient Israel
is transferred to the one true Israelite. God's ways have always run counter to the ways of man. Christ, the living Stone,
was rejected by man—his claim to messiahship was repu-
diated by Jewish religious leaders—but was chosen by God

and *precious to him*. The word for "precious" means "held in highest honor" or "esteemed."

5 As people continue to come to Christ by faith (note the present participle in the first phrase of v. 4), they, like he, can be said to be *living stones*. By the new birth they share his immortality. He is the capstone; they are the stones of which the edifice of the kingdom is built. The metaphor of the church as the temple of God is employed frequently by Paul (see Eph. 2:19-22; 1 Cor. 3:16-17; 2 Cor. 6:16). Note that it is by coming to Christ that people enter the church; it is not by entering the church that people are joined to Christ. We also learn from this figure that God intends his people to live out their lives in a constructive relationship with one another. Scattered bricks do not constitute a building. Scattered believers do not make a church.

The figures change quickly and the "living stones" of which the building is formed become the *holy priesthood* that carries out a sacred ministry within the building. As priests of a holy God (see 1:16) they are to offer *spiritual sacrifices*. Elsewhere we learn that such sacrifices include total commitment (Rom. 12:1), praise (Heb. 13:15), and practical concern for the needs of others (Heb. 13:16). These sacrifices are *acceptable to God through Jesus Christ*. Acts of high moral quality are not acceptable to God by virtue of their own intrinsic value. It is only as they are joined to the one great sacrifice of Christ that they receive divine approval.

Verses 6-8 form a parenthesis that expands the theme of the living Stone (v. 9 resumes discussion of the church as a priesthood). The metaphor has its roots in the Old Testament.

6 The first quotation (with minor modification) comes from Isaiah 28:16. God has laid in Zion a *chosen and precious cornerstone* (note the parallel with v. 4). "Cornerstone" probably refers to the final (or cap-) stone that ties the entire building together. Ephesians 2:19-22 pictures the church as built on the foundation of the apostles and prophets with Christ as the chief cornerstone. Those who trust in him *will never be put to shame*. God will never let them down. What he has promised he will bring to pass. *Zion*, as Peter uses the term, refers to the heavenly Jerusalem (see Heb. 12:22).

7a A literal translation of verse 7a is, "To you, therefore, who believe, is the honor." The honor to be shared by believers is the honor given to Christ in his exaltation. The *AV* translation, "He is precious" (followed by the *NIV* and others), is grammatically objectionable. Peter is not speaking of the intrinsic value of the cornerstone but of the honor that comes to believers because they have placed their trust in him (see Eph. 2:5-6).

7b, 8 Peter now quotes from Psalm 118:22 in support of his earlier statement (in v. 4) that the stone rejected by men has been chosen by God. It has become the very *capstone* of the entire building. Furthermore—and now the words are from Isaiah 8:14—this rejected stone is for unbelievers *a stone that causes men to stumble and a rock that makes them fall.* Here the picture is of a stone that lies in the way of travelers and causes them to stumble and fall. To refuse to acknowledge that Christ is the great messianic capstone of the temple of God is to stumble over the claim and fall. The ultimate help becomes a hindrance.

It is worth noting that all three of the Old Testament quotations in verses 6-8 are cited elsewhere in the New Testament (Rom. 9:33; Matt. 21:42; Acts 4:11). This suggests that the figure of speech was widespread in first-century Christianity.

Now comes an exceedingly important insight. Men stumble over the message *because they disobey.* Disobedience—not some philosophical or intellectual difficulty with the message itself—is the root cause of the unbeliever's downfall. People stumble because they *won't* believe, not because they *can't.* One of the central teachings of the Pastoral Epistles is that heresy stems from ethical failure (1 Tim. 1:5-6, 19; 2 Tim. 4:3). The final clause of verse 8 does not say that man's disobedience was *destined* but that his stumbling as a result of disobedience was determined beforehand. Phillips translates, "which makes stumbling a foregone conclusion."

9a Peter continues to draw from the Old Testament as
he sets forth the essential nature and purpose of the church.
The four descriptive phrases of verse 9 come from Exodus
and Isaiah. They are titles given to Israel in the Old Testament but transferred to the church in the New. The ease
with which this is accomplished demonstrates the conviction
of the early church that they were the true successors to
God's people of the former dispensation. An unbroken line
of faith extends from Abraham to the most recent convert to
the gospel message.

Like Israel of old, the church is a *chosen people* (see
Isa. 43:20). Their election brings them not only certain
privileges, but also some significant obligations. God told
Ananias that Paul was a "chosen instrument" whose ministry
would entail much suffering (Acts 9:15-16).

The church is also a *royal priesthood* (Exod. 19:6). Every
member is a priest because he has direct access to God. He
no longer needs a human intermediary to support his cause
with the blood of a slaughtered animal. Christ's sacrifice
once for all has opened the way into the most holy place (see
Heb. 7:26-28). Every ecclesiastical structure that places a
human representative between the individual believer and
God has forgotten the basic New Testament teaching of the
priesthood of all believers. This priesthood is "royal" because it belongs to and is in the service of the King.

Israel was a *holy nation* because it was set apart or consecrated to the service of God (Exod. 19:6). The word for
"nation" is *ethnos* (cf. the English "ethnic"); it originally
indicated a blood relationship. By the new birth all believers
become one race. Their distinguishing characteristic is that
they are "holy"—separate from sin and set apart for God and
his purposes. They are, therefore, a *people belonging to God*
(Isa. 43:21). The *AV* translation, "peculiar people," has raised
many an eyebrow because all too often Christians are "peculiar" in the wrong way. The *NEB* translates, "a people
claimed by God for his own." The value of an object sometimes lies in the fact that a person of special importance has
owned it. In a Philadelphia museum you can see a pair of

glasses that belonged to Thomas Edison. Their worth derives from ownership. We are people who belong to God. We are his possession. Our value comes from the fact that we belong to God—we are, in a special way, his purchased possession (see 1 Cor. 6:19-20).

9b, 10 The purpose of the church is to *declare the praises of him who called [it] out of darkness into his wonderful light.* Nowhere else in Scripture will you find a clearer statement of what the church is all about. Israel had been called out to bear witness to God (Isa. 43:10). In the New Testament this ministry of witness passed over to the church. To his disciples inquiring about the restoration of Israel, the resurrected Christ replied, "You will be my witnesses . . . to the ends of the earth" (Acts 1:8). That which is declared are the glorious qualities of God, especially as they are manifested in his great acts of history. He is the One who calls men "out of darkness into his wonderful light." Abraham was called from Ur of the Chaldees into the land of Canaan. The children of Israel were called from the darkness of Egyptian bondage into the light of the promised land. Jesus said, "The people living in darkness have seen a great light" (Matt. 4:16). Every serious believer knows that nothing less than the vivid contrast between darkness and light can do justice to the experience of coming to know Jesus Christ. In words supplied by Hosea, *Once [we] were not a people, but now [we] are the people of God* (Hos. 2:23). Once we lived apart from his mercy, but now we are enjoying his favor. It is against the background of this new relationship to God that we are able to proclaim his praises. Without a clear understanding of this basic transformation Christian witness falls flat and accomplishes little.

LIVING IN AN ALIEN SOCIETY (2:11-17)

11 Peter would have to be classed as an ethical realist. He was perfectly aware that although Christians may have committed themselves to a life of trust and obedience, the desires of the old man—the unregenerate self—continue to make their influence felt. A state of war exists between the new nature and the old. The seductive lure of evil remains even though the power to resist and overcome is available. So Peter says, *Abstain from sinful desires.* Weymouth has it, "Restrain the cravings of your lower natures." Salvation is deliverance from the *power* of the lower nature, not from its *presence.* Not until we are taken into glory and changed to be like him (1 John 3:2) will we be set free in an absolute sense from the temptation of sin. In the meantime we are to turn a deaf ear to the demands and desires of our lower natures.

These "fleshly lusts" are not simply the cravings of the physical body. The Greek word for "flesh" should be taken in the ethical sense of human nature in its state of sinful alienation from God. From Galatians 5:18-21 we learn that the works of the flesh include not only sexual immorality and debauchery, but hatred, jealousy, and selfish ambition as well. All of these *war against your soul.* Man's "soul" is not some separate component that helps make up his total being, but a way of designating one's self or individuality. Sinful desires have launched an all-out campaign against a person's best interests. It is a civil war, with the flesh in rebellion against the person himself and what is best for him. One of Satan's biggest lies is that God wants to keep us from all those things in life that are really fun. Paul Little refers to the caricature of God as a "celestial Scrooge" who, upon peering over the balcony of heaven and spotting a happy person, yells, "Now cut that out!" (*Affirming the Will of God,* p. 12). Actually the only things prohibited by God are those things which, if persisted in, bring heartache and suffering.

One reason we are to refuse to allow sinful desires to govern our conduct is that we are *foreigners and strangers in the world* (see 1:1, 17). Not only do we lack legal status ("foreigners"), but we will only be here for a short time ("strangers"). Sinful desires belong to this world. Our citizenship is in heaven (Phil. 3:20); therefore let us not submit to the alien control of our old natures.

12 And now the positive exhortation. *Live such good*

lives among the pagans that, though they accuse you of doing wrong, they may see your good deeds and glorify God on the day he visits us. Several items call for special note. "Good deeds," even though they may be misrepresented and defamed for the moment, are still the best answer to the opposition of a hostile world. We are challenged to prove by our conduct the intrinsic moral superiority of the Christian faith. Academic argument or defensive tactics designed to protect the truth are human ways to meet opposition. God urges us to take the offensive. Our weapons are good deeds— everyday expressions of the love of God in the give-and-take of actual living. This is how we ward off the accusations of those who despise us because they cannot tolerate the Lord we love (see John 15:18-25).

In Peter's day, and the years following, Christians were accused of such things as incest, cannibalism (the Lord's Supper), treason, and hatred of mankind. How useless it would have been to mount a defense item by item. Better to live in love and pray that God will enlighten those whose opinions stem from malice and prejudice. In time those who watch your good deeds may come to realize that your conduct is upright. This will result in their giving glory to God. The "day of visitation" could mean either the day of final judgment or the day when God "visits" each person who turns to him in faith. The latter interpretation has the contextual advantage: praise rises from a proper appreciation of good works.

13a   Peter calls upon his readers to *submit* themselves *to every authority instituted among men.* A literal translation of the Greek is "every human creature." This has been understood to mean "all human institutions" (*TCNT*), "every human creation" (*Rotherhem*), "every law of your government" (*LB*). The following verses show that Peter is talking about submission to kings and governors. Believers are to recognize civil authorities and submit to them. Being "strangers in the world" (v. 11) does not exempt them from compliance with the laws of the land. The same obedience to civil authority is taught by Paul in Romans 13:1-7.

Submission to authority for the Christian is said to be *for the Lord's sake.* Several things may be intended by this. Believers are to comply with the requirements of civil authorities because they (the latter) are divinely ordained (see Rom. 13:1-2, 4-5). Christ himself respected secular authority. By their obedience his followers will commend the Christian faith to others. Obviously, submission to secular authority was never intended to be taken in an absolute or unqualified sense. Occasions arise in which obedience to God overrules obedience to the state. For example, Peter and John were forbidden by the Jewish religious authorities to continue teaching in the name of Jesus. They answered, "Judge for yourselves whether it is right in God's sight to obey you rather than God. For we cannot help speaking about what we have seen and heard" (Acts 4:19-20). Peter in his letter is speaking about civil obedience in a normal situation.

13b, 14 Believers are to submit themselves to *the king, as the supreme authority.* In Peter's day the reigning authority was the infamous Nero. A Christian's obligation to obey the law does not depend upon the moral virtue of the leader. The term *governors* would include all intermediary authorities between the king and the people. They perform a double function. On the one hand, they *punish those who do wrong.* God has given to the civil magistrates the authority to punish antisocial behavior. Paul teaches that "the authorities that exist have been established by God" (Rom. 13:1). To disobey the law of the land is to disobey God. God is firmly committed to "law and order." While people may differ as to how far this authority may extend—for example, does God approve of capital punishment?—there is no question that appropriate methods of social control are divinely ordained.

Civil authorities also have responsibility to *commend those who do right.* They do this by recognizing noteworthy achievements and giving honor where it is due. Unfortunately this positive role of government gets less attention than its restrictive or punitive role.

15 This verse is somewhat parallel to verse 12 in which

good works are said to bring glory to God. Here we learn that *it is God's will that by doing good [they] should silence the ignorant talk of foolish men.* The best way to counter opposition is to live such a transparently good and honest life that no one will be able to mount a credible case against you. "Ignorant talk" is the chatter of uninformed persons. The "foolish" are those who condemn without reason the Christian and his faith. In time good works will silence all such empty verbal opposition. The Greek verb for "put to silence" is cognate to the word for "muzzle." Doing good muzzles foolish and thoughtless speech.

Note: some commentators link verse 15 with the exhortation of verse 13. This would read, "Submit to every authority because this is the will of God." It is better to take verse 15 as a parenthetical remark supporting good works as God's way of silencing idle talk.

16 We are told to *live as free men* but not to make our freedom "an excuse for doing wrong" (Goodspeed). Peter was concerned that believers should never use their citizenship in a higher commonwealth as an excuse or cover-up for questionable conduct. Freedom is never freedom to hurt or harm another. To the contrary, freedom releases us from every restraint that would keep us from doing the right. No contradiction exists between living as free men and living *as servants of God.* To acknowledge God as absolute sovereign is to experience the real meaning of freedom. George Mattheson wrote, "Make me a captive, Lord, and then I shall be free." Paul says that we have been "set free from sin and have become slaves to righteousness" (Rom. 6:18). Only in total submission can man realize maximum freedom.

17 This section concludes with four brief exhortations. Each indicates the proper attitude and relationship we are to maintain toward a specific social group (or person). As Christians we are to *show proper respect to everyone.* Each person has been created in the image of God and is worthy of appropriate recognition. Respect for human personality lies at the base of Western culture. Each individual has spe-

cific inalienable rights. The designs of society are never to
be carried out at the expense of the individual.

Second, the Christian is to *love the brotherhood of believers*. Love goes a step beyond respect. It is active concern
for the welfare of another. It not only recognizes merit in
another but it sacrifices itself for the benefit of others. Mutual
concern and active caring should be the hallmark of the
Christian community.

Furthermore, the Christian is to *fear God*. We are to
revere him for who he is. "The fear of the Lord," declared
the Psalmist, "is the beginning of wisdom" (Ps. 111:10). He
is worthy of our praise and deep devotion. The greatness of
his person should stir within us a sense of awe and wonder.

Fourth, we are to *honor the king*. As God's appointed
regent he serves the cause of social order and justice. As
such he deserves honor. If, from time to time, we are unable
to applaud the moral character or approve of the decisions
of a national leader, we should still honor the office he holds.

CALLED TO UNJUST SUFFERING (2:18-25)

18 Peter calls upon *slaves* to submit themselves to their
masters—not only to those who are kind but to the mean
ones as well. The word translated "slave" denotes a domestic
servant rather than a slave used in large-scale industry or
agriculture. At the time Peter was writing, slaves constituted
better than 50 percent of the population of major cities. Although their role in society varied from doctors and teachers
to the lowest and most menial occupations, they were nevertheless the property of their owners and could be tortured
or done away with at the pleasure of their masters.

The exhortation to *submit* was perhaps necessary because some Christian slaves who had learned the biblical
principles of justice were moved to repudiate openly their
lot in life. In the preceding paragraph Peter taught that all
believers should submit to civil authorities. Now he goes on
to encourage slaves to submit to their masters. This they are
to do *with all respect*. The Greek "in all fear" probably

means out of reverence to God whose control extends to every circumstance of life—even to their slavery. The *NIV* understands the phrase as mandating respect toward one's master (as in Eph. 6:5).

Submission is appropriate not only to those masters who are *good and considerate* (and many were) but also *to those who are harsh.* Christian decorum does not depend upon the worth of the person whose position grants him authority. Since God has established "the authorities that exist" (Rom. 13:1), it is proper to address each with dignity and reserve.

19 Peter writes that *it is commendable* when a man endures unjust suffering consciously aware of the presence and will of God. The word is "grace." Those who suffer unjustly find favor in God's eyes because their willingness to endure is an expression of gratitude for all that God has done for them. God's grace prompts the human response of gratitude. Apart from this insight, suffering is simply suffering. It becomes a gracious act when understood as part of the divine intention for man.

20 Peter here repeats the truth that to *suffer for doing good* wins God's approval. The point is strengthened by calling attention to the obvious fact that enduring a beating for having done wrong is of no merit. Behind Peter's words we can hear the teaching of Jesus in Luke 6:32-35, "If you love those who love you, what credit is that to you? Even 'sinners' love those who love them ..." (see Matt. 5:46-48). We all must bear the suffering we deserve. It is most extraordinary when an innocent person accepts unjust suffering with patience and equanimity. But then, Christians are expected to be extraordinary people.

21 The apostles were acutely aware that God was at work in their midst. Life was not a haphazard sequence of unrelated events. God had a plan, and he was carrying it out in the lives of his followers.

So Peter writes, *To this,* that is, to a life of patient endurance in times of unjust suffering, *you were called.* A profound sense of divine ordering controlled their understanding of life. God was not a religious decoration to adorn a secular lifestyle but the controlling center of life itself. Believers were not called to social prominence based on religious achievement but to bearing up under undeserved suffering.

The supreme motive for this unusual way of accepting abuse is that *Christ suffered for you*. It is because he suffered that we should be willing to meet opposition with serenity—a serenity born not from natural temperament or learned response but from the realization that Christ's followers will receive from the world the same opposition as did their master (John 15:18-26). Gratitude is the only appropriate response to the wonder of redemption.

In his suffering Christ has left us *an example*. The Greek word means literally, "something written underneath." Christ is our example in the sense that he furnishes us the pattern we are to trace. Specifically, the ideal is to be a "carbon copy" of him. Or, to change the figure, we are to *follow in his steps*. In the words of Thomas a Kempis' devotional classic, we are called to the "imitation of Christ." Through obedience and suffering we grow to be like him.

Five times in verses 22-25 Peter quotes from or makes allusions to Isaiah 53. Even though he was an eyewitness of the sufferings of Jesus, he knew no better way of expressing the ordeal than to use the prophetic language of the Old Testament prophet.

22   As a "lamb without blemish or defect" (1:19) Christ had *committed no sin* (see Isa. 53:9). He was faultless. Peter had traveled with Jesus for over three years. He had watched him in every sort of circumstance. He had seen him tired and tempted, misunderstood and misrepresented. Yet never did he do or say anything that was in the least way inappropriate for the Son of God. Both his inner life and his external conduct were absolutely without sin.

No deceit was found in his mouth because deceit is the sinful manipulation of another for personal advantage. It is foreign to the lexicon of love.

23   Peter now emphasizes the remarkable reserve of Jesus during the period of his final testing. The religious

leaders of Judaism *hurled their insults at him* by placing a
blindfold over his eyes, spitting at him, and striking him with
their fists, while taunting him to "prophesy!" (Mark 14:65;
see also 15:31-32). The Roman soldiers crowned him with
thorns and mocked him as king (Mark 15:17-20). Even those
passing by the cross in the time of his agony reviled him
(Mark 15:29-30).

How did he respond? With dignified silence. *He did not
retaliate* (see Mark 14:61; 15:5; Luke 23:9). His cause was
just: his suffering unjust. As the lamb of God he quietly bore
the penalty for the sins of mankind. Even his tormentors
were included within the circle of his forgiveness. "Father,
forgive them," he prayed, "for they do not know what they
are doing" (Luke 23:34).

Peter goes on to say that *when he suffered, he made no
threats.* It is worth noting that throughout verse 23 the Greek
text uses present participles and verbs in the imperfect tense.
This stresses that both the suffering of Jesus and his refusal
to respond stretched over a period of time.

From an ancient account (*The Passion of St. Perpetua*)
we learn that some early Christian martyrs found it difficult
not to deride their accusers. As Perpetua and her colleagues
passed by Hilarianus, their judge, they jeered, "Thou judgest
us, but God will judge thee." Not so Christ. "He made no
threats." Instead *he entrusted himself to him who judges
justly.* He knew that he was without sin and that God was
a righteous judge. There could be but one outcome. God,
the righteous judge, would vindicate him. Jesus, in a literal
sense, laid his life on the line. He faced death fully convinced that once his sacrifice for sin was complete God had
no option but to raise him from the dead. The conviction
that righteousness will be rewarded and evil punished provides the basis for committing oneself to a life of nonretal-
iation. A moral God must and will vindicate the righteous
sufferer.

24 *He himself bore our sins in his body on the cross.*
Few statements in the New Testament exceed this in theological import. The entire redemptive purpose of God comes

into focus in this one great act of eternal significance. On the lonely altar of a Roman cross the Son of God becomes the ultimate sacrifice. He carries in his own body the just penalty for our sin. He is at the same time both the priest who lays the sacrifice on the altar (in the Septuagint the Greek verb is commonly used of bearing a sacrifice and placing it on the altar) and the victim who is sacrificed. The One who knew no sin becomes a sin-offering for mankind (see 2 Cor. 5:21; Heb. 9:28). The validity of the Christian faith rests entirely on this central claim—that Christ suffered the full penalty for all the sins of man. As the lamb of God he took upon himself the entire punishment for sin and paid the just penalty by the gift of his sinless life.

And note the purpose of this remarkable act of selfless love. He gave himself *so that we might die to sins*. The NEB has it, "That we might cease to live for sin." His death was for us. Its purpose was to free us, to separate us from the power of sin over our daily lives. Freed from sin, we are able to *live for righteousness*. What we could never have done as slaves to sin we are now free to carry out (see Rom. 6:11-23). Our salvation is not a theoretical doctrine: it is genuine deliverance from the controlling power of sin. The purpose of the cross is ethical. Christ's death intends to change the way we actually live.

It is by the *wounds* of Christ (the scars left by a lash) that believers *have been healed*. We are cured from the debilitating effects of sin because Christ suffered on the cross on our behalf. How this could be is a divine mystery. Understanding will have to wait until another day. Meanwhile we accept it with thanksgiving.

25 Peter describes mankind as *sheep going astray*. The figure is taken from the Servant Song of Isaiah 52:13–53:12— "All we like sheep have gone astray; we have turned every one to his own way" (see also Ezek. 34:5-6; Matt. 9:36). Like sheep that wander off aimlessly man has left the path laid out for him by God. (For an excellent book that draws extensively on analogies involving both sheep and shepherd, see Philip Keller's *A Shepherd Looks at Psalm 23*.)

But now the situation is different. Those to whom Peter writes *have returned.* Literally the word means "to turn toward." It appears in second-century writers with the meaning "to return." In his natural state man *turns from* God and wanders into error. Healed by the redemptive activity of Christ on the cross, he *turns back* to *the Shepherd and Overseer* of his soul.

In biblical times the shepherd was responsible for guiding his flock to good pasture ("He makes me lie down in green pastures," Ps. 23:2) and protecting them from wild beasts.

In John 10 Jesus declares, "I am the good shepherd" (vv. 11, 14). It is to Christ, the good shepherd, that repentant believers turn for guidance and protection. As Shepherd he is also Overseer (the One "who keeps watch over your souls," Knox). The term is not a title, parallel with Shepherd, but a description of what the Shepherd does. He oversees the spiritual welfare of those for whom he is responsible.

③

FIRST PETER THREE

HOW TO GET ALONG WITH YOUR SPOUSE (3:1-7)

1 Human nature makes it difficult for people to submit to one another. It goes against the grain of self-interest. Yet society cannot exist without order. We remember the chaos in the time of the judges when "everyone did as he saw fit" (Judg. 17:6: 21:25).

Order implies submission for the common good. In Chapter 2, Peter counseled believers to submit to civil authority (2:13) and slaves to submit to their masters (2:18). In Chapter 3 he turns to relationships within the immediate family. Wives are to be *submissive to [their] husbands.* Some translations have, "to your own husbands," which reflects more accurately the Greek text and at the same time places submission in a slightly different light. The rule is softened by noting that a wife's responsibility is to her own husband, not just the man she happened to marry.

Submission does not imply inferiority. A wife willingly carries out the practical consequences that follow the responsible decisions of her husband. By her obedience she shows her respect for the divine ordering of human relationships. Obedience is not an admission that one's spouse is intrinsically superior.

There is great concern in our day for the status of women. Anything that smacks of subservience to the male is immediately labeled chauvinistic. In this particular period of history it is especially difficult even for many Christians to see the reasonableness of Peter's counsel.

In view of today's sensitivity about women's rights it is crucial that this section of Scripture (3:1-6) be interpreted in light of its first-century social context. Women at that time played a less prominent role in society. Generally speaking, they were poorly educated and extremely limited in their opportunities for cultural growth. In the ancient world girl babies were often left to die at birth. Submission to one's husband is more understandable in this context.

The principle of submission, however, has relevance far beyond the cultural setting of antiquity. It is an expression of social order. The God who brought order out of chaos in the natural world (see Gen. 1) desires order in the social order as well. Even Christ himself is eternally subject to God the Father (1 Cor. 15:28). In no case is the one who submits necessarily inferior (or superior) to the other. In Paul's great treatment of the subject he prefaces his instruction that wives should submit to their husbands with the broader admonition directed to all believers, "Submit to one another" (Eph. 5:21).

In the verses under consideration the submission of wives has a specific purpose. It is that unbelieving husbands *may be won over* (the Greek word means "to gain" and carries the idea of positive benefit). It seems that the church historically has had more believing women than men. Here we have a Christian woman with a pagan husband opposed to the Christian faith (the expression *do not believe* is actually "do not obey"; *TCNT* has, "if any of them reject the Message"). In this situation the believing woman is to submit to her husband, even if he is difficult to get along with (see 2:18), so that he may be won over not by *talk* but by *the behavior* of his wife.

Silent evangelism is a biblical principle. Situations develop where nothing but godly and chaste behavior can convince a spouse of the reality of the Christian faith. A man determined to disobey God cannot be won by harping on what he already knows but has decided to ignore. The rebel must be led to the truth by more subtle means than a daily recital of his sins. Obviously it does not follow that *all* evangelism should be carried out "without a word." Common sense and biblical example prevent that extreme. Note: translations that supply the definite article ("without *the* word") understand the verse to mean that in the situation described it is useless to appeal to "the Word" (that is, the gospel) since for the unbeliever the teaching of Christ has no authority.

2 The disobedient are won over when they see for themselves the *purity and reverence* of their wives. Living together will offer many opportunities to observe how a mature believing wife will react both to the routine of daily life and to the moments of crisis that inevitably rise.

3 Having brought up the subject of appropriate behavior for Christian wives, Peter now goes on to explain what constitutes real beauty. Some commentators think that the women of whom Peter writes were trying to win their husbands to Christ by adopting all the latest fashions of paganism. There is nothing in the text that suggests that this was the motivation for outward adornment, although it is certainly possible.

The real beauty of a Christian wife has little to do with *outward adornment*. Peter cites several examples of what he means by the term. *Braided hair* refers to elaborate coiffures worn by women of the Greco-Roman world. Juvenal, the Roman satirist, mocks the practice, noting that building the hair up tier upon tier makes the woman "as tall as Andromache [the mythological wife of a Trojan hero] in front, and behind she is shorter" (*Satire* iv). Clement of Alexandria said that sleep comes to such women with terror lest they should accidentally spoil their coiffures.

Pagan society was also given to *the wearing of gold jewelry and fine clothes*. Pearls were a favorite adornment of that time. Seneca tells of women who carried several fortunes in their ears. Lolia Paulina, wife of Caligula the Roman emperor, wore a dress covered with pearls and emeralds costing close to a million dollars. Undue concern for external appearance reveals preoccupation with the superficial. For believing women to become caught up in the craze of fancy hairstyles, expensive jewelry, and elegant dress is to miss what real beauty is all about.

4 Beauty, says Peter, arises from within. Christian women should display *the unfading beauty of a gentle and quiet spirit*—the "inner loveliness of the heart" (Norlie). It is significant that the only words used by Jesus to describe himself (as reported in the Gospels) were "gentle" and "humble" (Matt. 11:29). The beauty that God sees is the beauty of the inner person. It is *of great worth in God's sight.* He values what we are within, not how we appear without. Man judges by external appearances, God looks on the heart.

In a day when so much attention is given to outward appearance (and even the so-called counterculture is in bondage to its own dress code) the Christian church needs to be reminded that God's concern is with the hidden man of the heart. A gentle and quite spirit is the most elegant apparel the inner man can wear. Since it is of "great worth" to God, it needs to be prized by all who profess to love him.

5 Peter draws upon the submissive attitude of pious women of former days as an example of what it means to possess the inner beauty of a gentle and quiet spirit. The *holy women* of Old Testament days were not a few select saints. The word *holy* means "set apart." All devout women are set apart in the sense of not being totally involved in the secular nature of contemporary society.

Such women are described positively as those who *put their hope in God.* Hope is that sure conviction that God will bring to pass what he has promised. By quiet trust the women *used to make themselves beautiful.* In a day when "beauty" is regularly defined in terms of physical attractiveness, the idea of beauty of character is often forgotten. Qualities that please God seldom capture the fancy of man.

Specifically, the women of old *were submissive to their own husbands.* Out of obedience to God they became obedient to their husbands. Taylor says, "They fitted in with

their husband's plans" (*LB*). Bear in mind that ancient society considered women to be second-class citizens. They
were deprived of those advantages necessary for social ad-
vancement and prestige. Peter knew that their true "liberation" could never be achieved by an aggressive approach to
life. If society would learn the true value of the individual,
no single group would ever be abused by those in authority.
As the message of freedom in Christ permeates society, the
abuses of power will subside. This is real liberation.

In the meantime, however, women are to carry out their
role in society in the spirit of gentleness and submission.
This is the higher road.

6 Sarah is singled out as the model of submission. She
obeyed Abraham and called him her master. She placed
herself under his leadership. She accepted his decisions and
honored his judgment. The word *master* (or lord) was commonly used as a secular title of honor. It reflects Sarah's
respect for her husband. It does not suggest a cringing relationship of servant to master.

Women who follow the example of Sarah can be called
her daughters. They show by their conduct that they are of
the same nature. They *do what is right* (obey their husbands) and *do not give way to fear*; they "permit nothing to
make [them] afraid" (Montgomery). Throughout this entire
section (vv. 1-6) Peter seems to be addressing Christian
women married to husbands who "do not believe the word"
(v. 1). In such cases it is easy to see how anxiety would be
aroused. A Christian wife would have natural concern about
submitting herself to the mandates of a non-Christian husband. Nevertheless, this is what Peter advocates. Obviously,
there would arise situations when this would not be appropriate. Peter doesn't lay down a blanket rule to be followed
without exceptions. In general, however, the believing wife
is to concur with the wishes of her husband. This is what
Sarah and other holy women of old did.

7 Peter took six verses to explain the marital responsibilities of the wife. He now takes but one verse to discuss

the role of the man. This imbalance reflects the unfavorable lot of the women in ancient society.

Most writers feel that *in the same way* goes back to 2:17 with its general exhortation to "show proper respect to everyone." But 2:13 and 2:17 would indicate that proper respect is shown by appropriate submission. Thus in 3:7 "in the same way" suggests a consideration on the part of the man for his wife that matches her "submission" to his leadership.

Husbands are to treat their wives *with respect* for two reasons. First, they are *the weaker partner.* The reference is physical. Because the man possessed greater physical strength, the heavier tasks should fall to him. To neglect these would be to fail to show respect.

Secondly, men are to respect their wives because they are *heirs with [them] of the gracious gift of life.* The joys of marital companionship must be inherited by both or not at all. Neither can enjoy the full blessing of life unless the other shares. Here is another example of the personal benefit that comes from loving concern for another. God's plan is that by putting the welfare of the other first both parties will be blessed.

When men live considerately with their wives and treat them with respect, it follows that *nothing will hinder [their] prayers.* This can mean either that husbands' prayers are hindered when God sees the thoughtless manner in which they treat their wives, or that husband and wife cannot join in prayer when the relationship between them is strained. The latter is probably what Peter had in mind. Personal grievances between husband and wife make it impossible for them to join in effective prayer. In the context of the previous verses this impasse could result from the failure of the wife to live in submission or the failure of the husband to show proper respect.

LIVING IN HARMONY (3:8-12)

8 *Finally* brings us to the close of a series of exhortations that began at 2:11. Verses 8-9 summarize in general terms

what it means to be a mature Christian. Six characteristics are listed, followed by a supporting quotation from Psalm 34.

In the first place Christians are to _live in harmony with one another_. In the Upper Room Jesus prayed that all who would believe in him would be one as he and his Father were one (John 17:20-21). To live in harmony does not mean to have the same opinion on every subject. God is not advocating a drab uniformity for his church. Rather, harmony has to do with oneness of attitude. Harmony is created when the various parts of an organization are properly related to one another in the pursuit of a common goal. Unity is the necessary result of all members of the church living in obedience to the one Spirit who indwells the body.

This emphasis on unity runs throughout the New Testament. The church is a body made up of many members. Each member belongs to all the others (Rom. 12:4). Paul appeals to the divided Corinthian church to "agree with one another so that there may be no divisions" (1 Cor. 1:10). To the Ephesians he writes, "Make every effort to keep the unity of the Spirit" (Eph. 4:3; see also 1 Cor. 10:17; 12:12-31; 2 Cor. 13:11; Eph. 2:13-14; Phil. 1:27; 2:2; 4:2). It is important to God that the church reflect in society the basic unity that results from the presence of God in the lives of his children.

A second characteristic of Christian maturity is sympathy. _Be sympathetic_ means "suffer together with others." We immediately think of such verses as Romans 12:15 ("Rejoice with those who rejoice; mourn with those who mourn") and 1 Corinthians 12:26 ("If one part suffers, every part suffers; if one part is honored, every part rejoices with it"). Sharing the joys and the sorrows of life follows naturally from the experience of Christian unity. Like the spokes of a wheel, the closer each is to the hub the closer he or she is to others. Unity and compassion are virtues that wax or wane together. It is impossible to be sympathetic and selfish at the same time. And remember that salvation, among other things, is deliverance from the power of self over the life.

The charge to _love as brothers_ is based on the fact that

believers are all one family. Because God is our Father and has first loved us (1 John 4:19), we are encouraged and enabled to love one another. Brotherly love is the badge of Christian discipleship (John 13:35). In fact, anyone who does not love has not passed from death into life (1 John 3:14). A nonloving Christian is a contradiction of terms.

We need to resist the temptation to pass over this truth too quickly. Verses that teach the absolute necessity of love are as true as those which teach that Christ died for sins. We are prone to build theologies on the latter while sweeping under the rug the former. Careful and critical attention to *all* Scripture teaches is of crucial importance. Our theologies tend to omit ethical injunctions that embarrass us by their either/or quality. They are there for our benefit.

To *be compassionate* means "to be tenderhearted." The Greek word has the literal (and the vivid) meaning "with healthy intestines." The Hebrews associated the visceral region with the emotions and affections. To be moved with compassion was to be stirred in the inner man. Some writers hold that Peter is here talking about courage (we speak of a person as having the "guts" to do some daring feat). This interpretation is less likely in the present context.

Believers are also to be *humble.* The Greek concept of virtue had no place for humility. It was looked down on as a sign of weakness. The Christian regards humility as a virtue because it acknowledges human frailty and looks to God for help. It is a proper stance before the Sovereign God who created every living creature and sustains all life by an act of his will. In addition, God in Christ Jesus humbled himself even to the depths of a common criminal hanged upon a cross. By his humility Christ has once for all laid out the pattern for Christian maturity. Self-assertiveness is the opposite of what it means to be a child of God.

But humility is not a passive virtue. It is not the limp acceptance of whatever comes along. Humility is an active decision not to retaliate or pursue redress for personal grievance. Someone remarked that "humility is a trait so rare that when you realize you have it you've lost it." Humility is a

balanced view of man's relative significance over against
God himself and the entire created order.

9 Peter proceeds to tell us how to react to those who
treat us with contempt. We are not to repay *evil with evil or
insult with insult.* Man's natural instinct is to strike back.
Unjust treatment seems for the moment to justify retaliation.
Yet Jesus taught nonresistance. When struck on one cheek
we are to turn the other (Matt. 5:39-42). Not to return insult
for insult is contrary to human nature. But isn't that the essence of Christian conduct—acting contrary to our old and
fallen nature?

Not only does the Christian refuse to retaliate but he
also takes the positive step of repaying insult *with blessing.*
To bless means to speak well of another. The believer calls
down God's blessing even upon his enemies (Luke 6:27).
Since God himself bestows his benefits upon all men (Matt.
5:44-45), the sons of God must openly reflect their Father's
generosity.

Peter tells his readers that it was to this very thing (i.e.,
reacting to abuse with an outgoing love) that they *were called.*
God knew the injustice his followers would suffer. He also
knew that the answer to injustice was not to retaliate in kind.
Only the loving acceptance of personal abuse is strong enough
to overcome the evil that prompts it. Believers are called to
this kind of living.

There is, however, another reason why the Christian is
to respond to evil with love. It is in this way that he will
inherit a blessing. The blessing he pronounces upon another
will return as an inheritance from God. No man can make
God his debtor. Every act of righteousness is rewarded by
God, who delights in bestowing his favors upon all who
gladly obey him.

10 Peter now quotes from Psalm 34 in support of the
exhortation just given (vv. 8-9). The writers of the New Testament are heavily indebted to the Old Testament not only
for theological insight but also for imagery and vocabulary.
Their hearts and minds were steeped in the literature of the
Jewish faith. Many commentators feel that when Peter quotes

almost verbatim verses 12-16a of Psalm 34 it may indicate that the material had already found its way into early Christian hymnody or catechism.

There are two requirements for the person who would *love life and see good days.* "Life" in this context is not simply life beyond the grave, but life right here on this earth. The statement parallels Jesus' words in John 10:10, "I have come that they may have life, and have it to the full." God's promises are not for some future age alone. To have eternal life means in one sense to have already entered into the blessings of the eternal state. It is a quality of life that reaches back into our present existence.

The first requirement is that a man *must keep his tongue from evil.* James warns us of the tongue—"a restless evil, full of deadly poison" (Jas. 3:8). And Jesus taught that "out of the overflow of the heart the mouth speaks" (Matt. 12:34). The answer to a wicked tongue is not so much closer control as it is a new heart. The tongue merely gives expression to the inner man. Ultimately we control the tongue by allowing God to change the inner man.

The second requirement is that a man keep *his lips from deceitful speech.* Unfortunately man uses the gift of speech to mislead. God confused the language of man at Babel to prevent their attempt to achieve total independence. Natural man now uses language to confuse, and civilization becomes the moral equivalent of Babel.

11 But malice and deceit rob a person of the joy of life and the pleasures of human existence. The person desiring God's blessing must *turn from evil.* The word for "turn" means literally "to bend away from." The picture is of a man leaning or bending away from evil when it approaches. He wants to avoid it at all costs.

Turning from evil, man's desire must be to *do good.* He must *seek peace and pursue it.* He is to search for peace and go after it with all his heart. Jesus taught, "Blessed are the peacemakers, for they will be called sons of God" (Matt. 5:9).

12 How comforting it is to know that *the eyes of the Lord are on the righteous.* He looks with favor upon those

who follow the path of obedience. Nothing escapes his notice. Every act of kindness is noted and remembered. The
Psalm continues, *and his ears are attentive to their prayer.*
He also listens. He awaits the prayers of the righteous. Have
you ever thought of prayerlessness as leaving God waiting
at the place of prayer? He is there. His ears are attentive.
But where are we? The Greek preposition in the phrase "to
their prayers" is instructive. Literally the text says that God's
ears are "into" the prayers of the righteous. It is almost as if
he were bending down to hear more clearly the requests of
his children.

While God actively pursues the welfare of the righteous, his *face* is set *against those who do evil.* The person
who has decided to do evil rather than to pursue good has
placed himself beyond the help of God. God never forces
his love on man. It must be freely received. To reject God's
forgiveness is to experience the terrifying reality of being
rejected by him.

CONFESSING YOUR FAITH CAN BE
DANGEROUS (3:13-17)

13 Mention of "those who do evil" (v. 12) would remind
believers of the opposition they were beginning to experience. They would remember that Jesus had warned them
that they would be persecuted, imprisoned, and brought before civil authorities (Luke 21:12). But, Peter asks, *Who is
going to harm you if you are eager to do good?* The answer
is, No one! It is the same sort of rhetorical question asked
by Paul in Romans 8, "Who shall separate us from the love
of Christ?" (v. 35). The Christian will face opposition and
may suffer, but he cannot be harmed in any significant way.
Knocked about, Yes, but separated from that which really
matters, Never.

Note that the promise is intended for those who are
"eager to do good." The Greek text says, "If you become
zealots of the good." In Jesus' day there was a band of fa-
natically loyal nationalists called Zealots. No sacrifice was

too great for the cause of freedom. They were reckless patriots consumed by a passionate love for their native land. Peter is saying that believers are to love goodness with the same fervent intensity. A burning desire to do what is right is the sure indication that one has experienced the goodness of God. Those who love goodness are, by that very love, freed from the fascination of evil. "No man can serve two masters" (Luke 16:13).

14 Even if a Christian should *suffer for what is right*, he is *blessed*. Suffering that is specifically Christian—that is, comes as a result of doing that which is right in God's eyes— is not a burden to be borne but a blessing to be received with thanksgiving. The word *blessed* means "highly privileged." Weymouth says that such a person is "to be envied." While there is nothing particularly praiseworthy about enduring those pains and distractions which come to all men (sickness, distress, death), the sufferings that result from following Christ bring rich reward. Jesus said, "Blessed are those who are persecuted because of righteousness, for theirs is the kingdom of heaven" (Matt. 5:10).

Peter continues, *Do not fear what they fear*. This could mean, "Do not fear the same things they fear," but this would be unnecessary. More likely it means, "Do not fear their threats" (those things with which they would frighten you). To the Philippians Paul wrote that a lack of fear on the believer's part would be a sign to the enemy that *they* were the ones who would be destroyed (Phil. 1:28). "Perfect love drives out fear" (1 John 4:18), and those who zealously pursue a life of righteousness have little time to worry about what God may or may not allow to happen in their lives.

The only fear of any consequence in the life of the believer is the fear of God. Cranfield quotes Daniel Cargill, the Scottish covenanter who on the gallows ladder declared, "Lord knows I go up this ladder with less fear and perturbation than ever I entered a pulpit to preach" (*The First Epistle of Peter*, p. 82).

15 Rather than being *frightened* (the Arndt-Gingrich lexicon translates the clause "do not let yourselves be intimidated," p. 813), believers are to *acknowledge Christ as the holy Lord.* The *NIV* adds "holy" to emphasize that the word for Lord is the Greek equivalent of the Old Testament name for God. Christ is lord not simply in the sense of master but in the sense of the sovereign God of the Judeo-Christian revelation. (The *AV* follows inferior Greek manuscripts that read "God" rather than "Christ.")

To reverence Christ as Lord *in your hearts* does not mean that true religion is a private matter and therefore not to be discussed publicly. The following exhortation dispels that notion. It means, rather, that true reverence for God is first and foremost a matter of the inner man. Genuine faith must of necessity rise from the depths of personal experience. Lip service to creed and custom will fall short. Eternal issues are decided in the lonely reaches of the human heart.

One way to "give honor to Christ" (*NTBE*) is to be ready at all times to present a rational defense of the Christian hope. When Peter says *always be prepared to give an answer,* he may be reflecting upon his own failure when questioned by the maid in the courtyard of the high priest (John 18:17). The question confronted Peter suddenly and without warning, and he failed the test. Peter left the place of his denial and wept bitterly (Luke 22:62). The event undoubtedly etched itself deeply into his conscience.

Some writers think that Peter is directing his readers to get ready for a formal defense of their faith before a civil court. The Greek word translated "answer" is *apologia* (compare the English "apology") and is often used in legal settings. Wuest mentions that the word literally means "to talk off from" and suggests the imagery of an attorney talking his client off from a charge (*First Peter in the Greek New Testament,* p. 89). In 2 Timothy 4:16 Paul reports that no one came to his support in his first defense (*apologia*). The admonition is probably broader, however, and refers to any informal and spontaneous situation where the Christian might have occasion to speak on behalf of his personal faith.

Christians are to be ready to share *the reason for the*

hope they have. Cultivated Greeks thought that every intelligent man should be able to give a reasonable explanation for his point of view. Belief in Christ is not an irrational leap of faith. Given the resurrection, it is a necessary and logical conclusion. The reality of the resurrection is a matter of historical probability. It is subject to the methodology of historical research. Faith, as E. J. Carnell repeatedly insisted, is the resting of the mind in the sufficiency of the evidence.

Jesus' teaching in Mark 13:11 regarding not worrying about what you should say when brought to trial because the Holy Spirit will do the speaking is not a contradiction. Peter's emphasis is on preparedness; Jesus speaks of the occasion itself.

16 Christian witness is not only to be rational but it is to be carried out *with gentleness and respect.* Jesus was "gentle and humble in heart" (Matt. 11:29), and his cause is best promoted by the same spirit. An aggressive defense of the faith betrays a misunderstanding of what the faith is all about. Theological differences should be discussed in an atmosphere of respect for the intelligence and integrity of each party.

It is also important for the Christian witness to keep a *clear conscience.* The freedom that comes with an untroubled conscience is indispensable for an effective witness. Awareness of unconfessed sin undermines the credibility of the message.

Thus far Peter has said that the Christian witness must be prepared, rational, and gentle, maintain respect, and do it all with a clear conscience. As a result, *those who speak maliciously against your good behavior in Christ* will be *ashamed of their slander.* The quality of your life will demonstrate that their slanderous attacks were unwarranted. They will be put to shame by their actions. Here we have the same teaching that we encountered earlier at 2:12. The Christian answer to evil is to overcome it with good. Sin is a moral disease and needs to be healed. To combat evil with evil is to increase its fury. As Jesus the Lamb of God bore the sins of the world, we, his followers, are to accept whatever abuse may be involved in identifying with his cause.

17 It goes without saying that *it is better . . . to suffer for doing good than for doing evil.* This is especially so when *it is God's will.* It may seem strange to some that God could will suffering. It is perhaps more accurate to say that God wills to bring good out of suffering. The great hymnody of George Mattheson, the blind poet of Edinburgh, was certainly not unconnected with his physical disability. The believer is an overcomer in that the very obstacles that were intended for his defeat are the stepping stones to victory. Suffering issues in triumph, not defeat.

CHRIST AND THE SPIRITS IN PRISON (3:18-22)

18 We now come to a section of Scripture widely recognized as perhaps the most difficult to understand in all the New Testament. Before we examine the individual phrases, it will be helpful to look at the unit in its larger context.

In the previous verses (13-17) Peter has argued that within God's will it is better to suffer for doing good than doing evil. This kind of suffering has positive benefit (v. 14). Christ himself suffered and died unjustly, but was raised in triumph. As the judgment of God fell upon the ancient world in the time of Noah and only those who had taken refuge in the ark were saved, so the judgment of God for the sins of man fell on Christ and only those who by faith (symbolized by baptism) take refuge in him are brought through the flood of divine retribution.

There should be no break at the beginning of Chapter 4. Since Christ's suffering placed him beyond the reach of sin (he died *for* sin and *to* sin), we who believe are to arm ourselves with the same attitude. Our lives are to be spent not in the grip of human desire, but in doing the will of God (4:2).

Now for some of the details. Verse 18 gives us the doctrine of the atonement in as succinct a statement as you will find anywhere. *Christ died for your sins* is a theological declaration that belongs to the earliest preaching of the primitive church. In 1 Corinthians 15:3 Paul acknowledges that he has passed on to them as of primary importance the message that "Christ died for our sins." This short credal clause contains both history and theological interpretation. No one would contest the fact that Christ died. That was historically verifiable. What was genuinely significant was that he died for our sins. This follows not only from his own teaching (see Mark 10:45) but from the historical fact of the resurrection. By being raised from the dead he was "decisively declared Son of God" (Rom. 1:4, Goodspeed).

Peter points out that this death was *once for all.* Unlike the priests who day by day offered the same sacrifices, which were unable to take away sin, Christ "offered for all time one sacrifice for sins" (Heb. 10:11-12). This demonstrates not only the superiority of Christ's sacrifice but its absolutely unique role in God's redemptive plan. All previous sacrifice pointed ahead to this final all-encompassing act of self-surrender (Heb. 7:26-28).

That Christ's death was *the righteous for the unrighteous* is in keeping with the vicarious or substitutionary nature of the sacrificial system. The lamb slain as a sin-offering had to be without defect (Lev. 4:32). Its life was taken for the sins of the people. John the Baptist declared of Jesus, "Look, the Lamb of God, who takes away the sin of the world" (John 1:29). Strange as it may seem to modern man, God's way of dealing with sin was to place the full consequences of human rebellion upon his sinless Son. The Righteous One is sacrificed for the unrighteous many.

Peter tells his readers that the purpose of Christ's death for the unrighteous was *to bring [them] to God.* In the Greek version of the Old Testament the verb is often used of the ritual act in which a sacrifice is made to God (see Exod. 29:10) and in situations where individuals are consecrated to God's service (see Exod. 29:4; Lev. 8:24). Both of these ideas may be in view here. By his sacrifice Christ brings us to God and consecrates us to his service (see Eph. 2:18). He is the priest who opens the way to the presence of God (see Heb. 4:16; 7:25).

Next we learn that Christ was *put to death in the body but made alive by the Spirit.* This translation obscures two things. First, the words "body" and "spirit" are parallel and should be translated in the same manner (both are in the dative case and the *NIV's* "*in the* body . . . but . . . *by the* Spirit*"* is misleading). Second, the capital S on "Spirit" interprets the word to mean the Holy Spirit. In other words the clause is made to say that Jesus died physically but was resurrected by the Holy Spirit.

While this theology is certainly orthodox, it is not what the text actually says. Flesh and spirit represent two spheres of existence or two successive conditions of Christ's human nature. Romans 1 tells us that Christ was a descendant of David "according to the flesh" but by his resurrection was declared Son of God "according to the spirit" (Rom. 1:3-4). The point that Peter makes is that by means of the resurrection Christ passes into a new and fuller life. Previously he had experienced the limitations of physical existence. Now he enjoys the freedom of a spiritual mode of existence.

19 It was in this spiritual state (the *NIV's through whom* results from a misunderstanding of "spirit" in v. 18) that Christ *went and preached to the spirits in prison.* The first problem is to identify the spirits. Since they are said to have disobeyed during the period when the ark was being built, many commentators understand them to be the generation that perished in the Flood. Genesis 6 tells us that wickedness had become so great by that time that God in his grief decided to wipe mankind from the face of the earth (vv. 5-7).

Normally, however, the word *spirit* in the New Testament denotes a supernatural being whether good or evil. Hebrews 1:14 speaks of angels as "ministering spirits," and Luke 8:28 identifies a demon as an "evil spirit." It is unnecessary to connect this passage with the sin of the "sons of God" in Genesis 6:1-4 and posit an unholy alliance between angels and women. The imprisoned spirits of 1 Peter 3 are the fallen angels of 2 Peter 2:4 who are held for judgment in the gloomy dungeons of Tartarus, that subterranean place of detention which according to Greek thought was on a level below Hades.

What does it mean that Christ "preached" to these fallen angels? (Those who take the spirits to be men sometimes use this verse to support the doctrine of a second chance for salvation beyond this life.) The Greek New Testament uses two words for preaching. The more common word stresses the content of the message; it is good news. The other word, which is used here, emphasizes the act of preaching. It is best translated "to proclaim." The *NEB* has, "and in the spirit he went and made his proclamation to the imprisoned spirits." Christ's proclamation to the fallen angels was not the offer of a second chance but the announcement of his complete and final victory over the power of sin and Satan. By his death and resurrection Christ had "disarmed the powers and authorities" and "made a public spectacle of them, triumphing over them by the cross" (Col. 2:15). The victory was proclaimed to the fallen angels during the period between the death of Jesus and his resurrection three days later. At the end of time every knee shall bow before him— even those "under the earth"—and every tongue shall confess his Lordship (Phil. 2:10-11).

20 The spirits are said to have *disobeyed long ago when God waited patiently in the days of Noah while the ark was being built.* This seems to make the disobedience of the angels contemporaneous with the period during which the ark was under construction. What we are probably to understand is that although the angels fell from their exalted place long before the time of Noah, they were still in a state of disobedience when the similarly disobedient human race was trying the patience of God—that is, when the ark was being built.

Only a few people, eight in all, were saved through water. To be "saved through water" in this context means either that Noah and his family were brought safely through the Flood or that by means of the Flood they escaped the judgment that fell upon the world. In the following verse the

—57—

Flood is said to symbolize baptism. This inclines many commentators to take the phrase "through water" in the instrumental sense. The parallel then would be between baptism that now saves and the Flood that saved or preserved at that time. The problem is to explain in what sense the Flood "saved." Was it not the ark that saved them from the Flood? The usual answer is that the water preserved them by floating the ark and bringing it through to safety.

It is better to take the text to mean that Noah and his family were brought through the Flood safely by the ark. The analogy in the following verse is loosely constructed and should not exercise undue influence on the interpretation of the entire section. Literature often demands more freedom than its interpreters are willing to allow.

21 The early church often interpreted Scripture typologically. Persons, things, and events of the Old Testament were held to be types of their New Testament counterparts. The New Testament itself provided the precedent for this practice. For example, Hebrews 9:24 says that the earthly temple was merely a copy of the true (heavenly) one. Romans 5:14 states that the first Adam was a pattern (*typos*, "type") of the one to come (Christ). An antitype is that which is foreshadowed by the type.

Peter now says that *water symbolizes baptism*. The flood in the time of Noah foreshadowed the baptismal water of the Christian era. The antitype (baptism) was prefigured by the type (the Flood).

The problem arises with the next clause, which says that baptism *now saves you*. How does baptism save? Is Peter teaching what came to be known in the early church as baptismal regeneration? The answer is clear when we realize that the statement does not stand alone but is completed by the final clause of the verse, *by the resurrection of Jesus Christ*. Not the act but the event that lies behind what the act symbolizes is the only meritorious basis for salvation. Peter breaks off for a moment to guard against a misunderstanding of what he means by baptism. It is by virtue of the resurrection that an identification with Jesus Christ (symbolized by baptism) brings salvation. Apart from the resurrection there could be no salvation.

Lest anyone think that the mere act of baptism has any saving power, Peter qualifies his statement in two ways. First, baptism is not simply *the removal of dirt from the body.* Physical washing does not cleanse the soul. Secondly, baptism is (that is, symbolizes) *the pledge of a good conscience toward God.* Some writers understand this as the baptismal candidate's prayer to God for a clean conscience (e.g., Moffatt; Goodspeed translates, "the craving for a conscience right with God"). Others hold it to be the candidate's pledge or vow to God that he will maintain a good conscience. This is supported by the fact that the word *pledge* was used as a technical term in making a contract. In either case, the important point is that the physical act of baptism has no saving power. Salvation comes as a response to man's inner relationship to God. It is based not upon what man does but upon *the resurrection of Jesus Christ.* Had Christ not been raised there would be no hope of salvation at all (see 1 Cor. 15:12-19). The act of baptism would have been vain and meaningless.

22 In verse 19 we learned that Jesus "went . . . to the spirits in prison." The same verb is now used to chronicle the next stage in the Lord's postresurrection activity. He *has gone into heaven.* His ministry on earth is complete.

In heaven Jesus is said to be *at God's right hand.* The right hand is the place of honor. When Bathsheba approached Solomon on behalf of Adonijah, a throne was brought for her and placed at the king's right hand (1 Kings 2:19; see also Ps. 110:1). To be at God's right hand would be to occupy a place of supreme privilege and authority. That Stephen in Acts 7:55-56 sees the Son of Man *standing* at the right hand of God and Paul in Colossians 3:1 writes that Christ is *seated* in the same place should cause no concern. The significance is theological. In all three instances it is the honor of being at God's right hand that is important.

Angels, authorities and powers are in submission to the

victorious Christ. These terms appear to be technical names for various divisions of supernatural beings. There was considerable speculation among Jewish thinkers of the day with respect to angelic orders. If Peter is speaking of evil beings, then they would correspond to the "powers and authorities" that were disarmed and made a public spectacle by the triumph of the cross (Col. 2:15).

FIRST PETER FOUR

BEING A CHRISTIAN IS A DEATH AND LIFE AFFAIR (4:1-6)

1 Following an unusually complicated digression into the side issue of preaching to the spirits in prison and baptism (3:18b-22), Peter returns to the subject of Christ's death and its purpose for believers. *Therefore*, he writes, *since Christ suffered in his body, arm yourselves also with the same attitude.* The suffering of Christ does not refer exclusively to the physical pain of Jesus' last hours on earth. It includes all the suffering of every sort that he bore as a result of the incarnation. This suffering reached its peak in his spiritual separation from God the Father in those dark hours upon the cross. "My God, my God, why have you forsaken me?" (Mark 15:34) is the essence of Christ's suffering "in body" (the *NIV* adds "his," which places undue stress on the physical aspect of Christ's suffering).

Christ met sin in mortal combat and emerged victorious. We are to adopt the same attitude. The insight we share is that *he who has suffered in his body is done with sin.* Christ died for sin and is therefore freed from the claims of sin and death. Romans 6 is Paul's treatment of the same truth. The believer is united with Christ in his death (6:5) and therefore alive with him in his resurrection (6:8). Death has brought freedom from sin (6:7); therefore the believer is now to consider himself dead to sin and alive to God (6:11).

So Peter reasons, Since Christ died to sin (and baptism

signifies our union with him in death and resurrection), we are to arm ourselves with the understanding that we also are done with sin. This is to be our attitude and outlook. Note that this interpretation takes the last clause of verse 1 as providing the content of the previous phrase, "the same attitude." The *NIV* joins the final clause with "because" and makes it supply the *reason* for arming ourselves. This is grammatically acceptable but less probable. Some commentators take the final clause of verse 1 as teaching the cleansing power of bodily suffering. While physical suffering sometimes serves as a psychological catharsis, this is hardly what Peter is teaching. Other commentators refer the final clause to Christ himself. It is better to take it as a spiritual axiom the truth of which was demonstrated by the death and resurrection of Jesus Christ and which now serves to arm the believer with the appropriate attitude in his daily battle against sin. Peter would agree with Paul's rhetorical, "Shall we go on sinning so that grace may abound? By no means! We died to sin; how can we live in it any longer?" (Rom. 6:1-2). To be joined to the One who died for sins is to have given up sin as a way of life.

2 Verse 2 states the purpose for arming ourselves with the insight just expressed. We consider ourselves dead to sin in order that we may *live the rest of [our] earthly life* in a certain way. Peter is not simply pointing out that we are to live in a certain manner during the years of our life that remain. The expression implies that the end is not far off. At least a period of time remains. We are to live it not *for evil human desires, but rather for the will of God.* TCNT translates, "guided not by human passions, but by the will of God." Norlie has, "Not in satisfying human appetites but in doing God's will." The point is clear. Recognizing that sin has neither the right nor the power to control those who in Christ have paid its debt, the believer may now live according to an entirely new principle. He is freed from the dominance of evil human desires and enabled to live according to the will of God.

3 The contrast between appropriate Christian conduct

and the lifestyle of paganism is sharp and clear. Believers had *spent enough time in the past doing what pagans choose to do*—then follows a list of vices similar to those mentioned by Paul in Romans 13:13 and Galatians 5:19-21. Such lists developed as part of the preaching activity of the early apostles. They sketch a picture of first-century paganism that leads us to believe that their twentieth-century counterparts have made little progress in the art of sinning.

With a touch of irony Peter writes that the time that has already been lost has been more than enough to have carried out the deliberate purpose (note how the word is used in Acts 27:43) of the pagan world. The will of the Gentiles (v. 3) is contrasted with the will of God in the previous verse (v. 2). These two stand at opposite poles of morality and ethics. They are radically distinct. God's desires for man are entirely different from the desires of an unredeemed society.

Now follows a vivid and detailed description of "what pagans choose to do." They live out their lives in *debauchery, lust,* and *drunkenness.* Each of the Greek nouns is plural, suggesting "all kinds" or "continual acts" of each vice. "Debauchery," according to one writer, refers to "open outrages against decency." In verse 2 the word for "lust" was translated "evil human desires." "Drunkenness" is inevitably a part of any milieu of sexual and social improprieties.

In the *Living Bible orgies* and *carousing* are called "wild parties" and "drinking bouts" ("hard drinking," says the *TCNT*). The final term, *detestable idolatry*, refers to idol worship, which was forbidden by Mosaic law (see Acts 10:28 for the only other use of the word "detestable" in the New Testament). The meaning, however, may be broader and include the laws of nature and conscience (in classical Greek it meant forbidden by natural law). The inclusion of this final term in the list of pagan characteristics suggests that sexual and alcoholic excesses were very much a part of non-Christian religious practices.

4 Those in the first-century world who became Christians would necessarily withdraw from the kind of social profligacy just described. This separation on the grounds of moral conduct seemed _strange_ to the unbeliever. Former companions were genuinely surprised when converts to the Christian faith would no longer _plunge with them into the same flood of dissipation._ The phrase pictures evil men racing headlong into a rushing torrent of wild debauchery. The Berkeley version calls it "unbridled dissipation," and the _NTBE_ has "the violent wasting of life." The final term occurs in a slightly different form in the account of the Prodigal Son, who spent his substance in a far country in "riotous living" (Luke 15:13, _AV_).

The sensitivities of the pagan world had become so dulled by their own crude manner of living that they were unable to understand why anyone would exchange a hedonistic lifestyle for the moral restrictions of some religious sect. What could be gained from it? Not only were they surprised, but they turned hostile as well. Christians were held to be a queer group of killjoys. Their very presence was resented by their profligate neighbors. This dramatic difference in moral standards led with increasing frequency to active persecution. That is why, Peter says, _they heap abuse on you._ The Greek word is _blasphēmeō_, from which we get the English "blaspheme." While it sometimes occurs in contexts where it means to speak with disrespect of God and sacred things (see Matt. 9:7), here it means to malign or slander and is directed toward believers (see Rom. 3:8). Such treatment should come as no surprise to those who had been warned by Jesus that they would be persecuted and hated by all nations (Matt. 24:9). Pagans were astonished that believers who had formerly been their companions in reckless living would no longer join them in the pursuit of pleasure. They expressed their surprise by slander and verbal abuse. Kelly calls it a "crude outlet for the pagan's astonishment."

5 The heathen world, however, will not get off scot-free. They will face judgment for the way they have spent their lives. They will have to _give account to him who is ready to judge the living and the dead._ Whereas believers must for the moment endure the slander of pagan society, those who pursue wickedness will on the day of judgment

come face to face with the righteous Judge. Jesus taught that on the day of judgment "men will have to give account [same phrase] . . . for every careless word they have spoken" (Matt. 12:36). Since "the Father judges no one, but has entrusted all judgment to the Son" (John 5:22), Jesus is the judge. Not to have taken him as Savior means to meet him as judge.

To be "ready to judge" does not mean to be eager to pronounce judgment. Jesus is ready in the sense that by knowing and seeing all he is perfectly equipped at every moment to bring a fair and impartial judgment of man's waywardness. "The living and the dead" emphasizes the universal scope of judgment. No one will escape, even by death. The expression became a part of the earliest creeds and came to refer both to those who would be alive and those who had already died at the time Christ returns.

6 This verse is obscure and has therefore been interpreted in a number of ways. *For this is the reason the gospel was preached* does not refer back to the preceding verse as if Peter were presenting a reason for the proclamation of the gospel. The gospel is not preached so Christ will have a basis for judging the living and the dead. The phrase points forward. The purpose of the preaching is that although believers share in the common sentence on mankind (death) they may live toward God in the spirit.

The verse as a whole is normally understood in one of three ways. First, Christ is held to have descended into Hell at death and preached to those who had never heard the gospel or those who had refused its offer of salvation. Although they had been *judged* (the verb is past tense), they still may *live* (present tense). This interpretation is favored by liberal theologians who wish to extend the boundaries of salvation but is contradicted by the clear teaching of Scripture that "man is determined to die once, and after that to face judgment" (Heb. 9:27)

Secondly, "the dead" are taken as the spiritually dead. Reference is made to such verses as Ephesians 2:1 ("you were dead in your transgressions and sins") and Colossians 2:13 ("you were dead in your sins"). There are two basic problems with this interpretation: (a) "Dead" in verse 5 means physically dead. It would be most unusual to use the same term in two widely different ways within the same unit of discourse. (b) The tense of the main verb "was preached" places the action in the past and says nothing of those who are unbelievers at the present time. If a general truth were being set forward, we would expect a statement to the effect that the gospel *is being preached* (present tense) to those who are dead in their sins.

The most reasonable way to understand the verse is to take it as referring to Christian converts *who are now dead*; that is, at some time after having heard and received the gospel they died. The early church had some concern about believers who had died before the Lord could return. Paul writes to the Christians at Thessalonica telling them not to grieve because when Jesus returned he would raise the dead at the same time he took the living (1 Thess. 4:13-17).

The purpose of preaching is laid out in two closely parallel clauses. It is *so that*

they might be judged
      according to men
      in regard to the body
but live
      according to God
      in regard to the spirit.

The threefold relationship and rhythmic balance between the clauses suggest that the entire unit was part of an early Christian creed. If this is so, we may expect it to be rich in theological truth and central to the early church's understanding of what it meant to be a follower of Christ.

To be "judged according to men in regard to the body" means to share in the judgment passed upon all physical life—that is, death. Paul teaches that death entered the world through the sin of Adam and passes to all men (Rom. 5:12). Physical death is a universal reality. The *NEB* translates, "In the body they received the sentence common to men." Although destined for physical death the believer is enabled to live in the spirit in his relation to God. "Body" and "spirit" are the two spheres of existence. They stand for life within its physical limitations, and life in its spiritual dimension. "According to men" and "according to God" relate to body and spirit respectively. A similar antithesis occurs in the description of Christ in Romans 1:3-4: he is a descendant of David "according to flesh" and Son of God "according to spirit" (literal translation). Peter's point is that the purpose of the gospel is that although man is marked for death, by responding to the gospel he may live unto God.

HOW TO LIVE IN THE FAMILY OF GOD (4:7-11)

7 Mention of judgment (vv. 5-6) turns Peter's thoughts to the imminence of the end. *The end of all things is near.* The Greek word for "end" is rich in theological meaning. To say that the end of all things has drawn near is not simply to announce that the close of history has arrived. The *telos*, or end, is also the goal toward which history moves—that which gives meaning to the entire process of events. The end of history in the sense of time is important only in that it is the occasion for the realization of the goal of history in the sense of purpose or outcome.

Peter clearly states that the end is near. He shares this view with others in the early church. Paul told his readers in Rome to wake up because the day was almost there (Rom. 13:11-12). To the Corinthians he wrote, "The time is short. . . . This world in its present form is passing away" (1 Cor. 7:29-31). John declared, "This is the last hour" (1 John 2:18), and the author of Hebrews counseled believers to encourage one another "as you see the Day approaching" (Heb. 13:11). In the next to last verse of the New Testament the resurrected Christ promised, "I am coming soon" (Rev. 22:20).

The obvious question is, Why hasn't the end come? Almost two thousand years have passed and life continues on. What shall we say about this New Testament emphasis on the imminence of the end?

Some hold that the early church was mistaken in their confidence that Christ would soon return. This, however, is to say that Scripture cannot be trusted. Others note that God's method of reckoning time is distinctly different from ours. With God a day is like a thousand years (see 2 Pet. 3:8). Thus Peter can say to us that the end is near because only two days (read "two thousand years") of _God's time_ have passed since he wrote. The mandates that follow, however, are based upon the nearness of the end as we normally reckon time. That Christ would come within two or three thousand years would supply no sanction for ethical conduct in Peter's day.

Still others claim that since death is never far away, the end _for each of us_ is always imminent. True, but this is not what the verse is saying. "The end of all things" is not a veiled phrase that means "the last moment of each of your lives." It is _the end_—the climax of human history that reveals the goal and purpose of the entire sequence of events from Adam to the return of Christ.

The early church was convinced that with Christ the last days had begun. God's rule on earth had been established. Jesus said, "If I drive out demons by the finger of God [and Jesus had just exorcised a demon from a dumb man], then the kingdom of God has come to you" (Luke 11:20). Paul wrote that the examples in the Old Testament were for those of his day "on whom the fulfillment of the ages has come" (1 Cor. 10:11). Hebrews 1:2 speaks of "these last days" in which God has spoken to us by his Son. Since the last days began with Christ, all that remains is what has been called "the epilogue to history." The end has drawn near because the last days _have begun._ This calls for a radically different way of living. In whatever time remains believers are to live with a heightened sense of eternal values.

Peter now tells his readers how to live in view of the fact that the last days have already begun and the end is near. First, they are to be _clear-minded and self-controlled._ The first expression means to be of sound mind, reasonable, and sensible. Knowledge of the end could lead some to become excited and act unreasonably. The word is used of the Gerasene demoniac who after his healing was found by his countrymen dressed and "in his right mind" (Mark 5:15).

The original meaning of the second term was to be sober (in contrast to being drunk). The cognate adjective in classical Greek described a teetotaler, one who drank no wine. Peter is calling on his readers to live soberly. In this context he is emphasizing sobriety of judgment. In the light of eternity believers must live out their days in a reasonable and temperate manner. Balance is necessary *so that [they] can pray.* Perhaps Peter remembers that sad occasion in the Garden of Gethsemane when with others he was sleeping rather than watching and praying (Mark 14:37-38). His carelessness in that time of testing played a major role in his subsequent denial.

8 *Above all*, Peter writes, *love each other deeply.* The highest priority for Christian living is love. God is love, and everyone who loves has been born of God. Brotherly love is the proof that we have passed from death unto life (1 John 4:16, 7; 3:14). Christian love is not a warm feeling. It is the determination to place the rights and welfare of others ahead of concern for oneself. The word translated "deeply" suggests intensity or earnestness. The root idea is "to be stretched." One Greek writer used it to describe a horse at full gallop. This is the way we are to love each other—strenuously and fervently. The primacy of active concern for others is the central thrust of New Testament ethics (see 1 Cor. 13; Gal. 5:13-15; Jas. 2:8; etc.).

We are to "love each other deeply" because *love covers over a multitude of sins.* This proverbial statement is often interpreted in the sense of its Old Testament counterpart. "Hatred stirs up dissension, but love covers over all wrongs" (Prov. 10:12). That is, our love for one another will cover over or hide the shortcomings of each other. Others, taking into account the eschatological context, interpret the statement to mean that if believers love one another God's love will cover their own sins. God's mercy is extended to those whose love for others is genuine. Matthew 25:31-46 has often been referred to as an illustration of this principle. The kingdom has been prepared for those who feed, clothe, and visit the needy. I am inclined to take the verse in the former sense. We are to love one another because love helps us overlook the faults of others. The *TCNT* translates, "Love throws a veil over countless sins."

9 One practical way to love is to *offer hospitality to one another.* In the early days when Christianity was spreading rapidly there were very few inns. Those that were had bad reputations both for the accommodations they offered and the low level of morality they encouraged. It was therefore imperative for the spread of Christianity that believers provide lodging for itinerant preachers and teachers (see Heb. 13:2). This could obviously become a burden in some cases. The necessity of meeting in homes for worship (someone noted that it took three centuries to design a building so inept that it could be used but one day a week!) and the large number of people whose business kept them on the road put a severe strain on hospitality. Peter exhorts his readers to carry out their Christian obligation *without grumbling.* Kelly cites an Italian proverb, "A guest is like a fish—after three days he stinks." However that may be, hospitality is to be shown without resentment. To serve the needs of others is to serve Christ himself (Matt. 25:35).

10 The close relationship between verses 9 and 10 suggests that hospitality was considered a spiritual gift. The concept was not restricted to the more obvious gifts of teaching and preaching. It included (according to Rom. 12:6-8) such abilities as serving, encouraging, giving, governing, and showing mercy. Peter writes that *each one should use whatever spiritual gift he has received to serve others.* This implies that every believer has received some gift. No member of the local congregation can say, I have nothing to offer. Each person's responsibility is to determine his gift and exercise it for the common good of others. Paul's well-known analogy in 1 Corinthians 12 is that of the body. Because the foot is not the hand, it does not follow that it is not a part of the body (1 Cor. 12:15). Nor can the eye say to the hand, "I don't need you" (1 Cor. 12:21). God has distributed among the membership of every believing community all the gifts necessary for their spiritual growth and activity. The Greek word for "gift" (*charisma*) stems from the word for grace (*charis*). God's gifts are freely and graciously given.

Each believer serves others by *faithfully administering God's grace in its various forms.* Williams translates, "good trustees of God's many-sided favour." The Greek trustee or steward was responsible for managing the estate of his master. Entrusted into his care were domestic affairs, supervision of tenants, and the distribution of wages. It was a responsible position. The steward himself owned no part of that over which he exercised control. He was fully accountable to his master for the way in which he carried out his task.

The final clause of verse 10 is often misunderstood to mean that as stewards we minister the grace of God. The grace of God is not the object of our stewardship but the basis upon which we were called to serve as stewards.

11 Peter now turns to two major types of Christian ministry, the spoken word (preaching and teaching) and acts of kindness and concern. *If anyone speaks, he should do it as one speaking the very words of God.* The word *logia* ("words") has a rather special history. It was used in heathen cultures of messages or short sayings held to have originated with the gods. It was used of revelations made to Moses in the Old Testament (see Acts 7:38). It came to be used of Scripture and the charismatic utterances of New Testament prophets.

Peter is saying that those who speak within the church are to deliver their messages as "words spoken by God Himself" (Stibbs). Genuine preaching involves a miracle. Although the words are spoken by man, the message is God's. God himself enters the communication process and uses the words of man as an instrument to convey his own truth to the hearers. Every preacher of the Word ought to be fully aware of the supernatural transaction taking place when he proclaims the Word of God.

The second example of the proper use of spiritual gifts relates to deeds rather than speech—*if anyone serves* (the verb is cognate to our English word "deacon"). The role of the deacon is to minister to the needs of the congregation. Those who serve are to carry out their task *with the strength God provides.* He is the One who makes possible all our serving. He grants us the strength to carry out the task. The word translated "provides" originally meant to underwrite personally the expenses of a choir for a public festival. It carries the idea of lavish support. The acts of kindly concern we do for the needy are made possible by God's abundant supply of strength.

The motive and purpose for speaking and acting in this manner is that *in all things God may be praised.* The full scope of Christian activity should bring glory to God. Speaking the oracles of God and carrying out his concern for man in the strength he supplies leads people to praise and honor God. This praise is said to be given *through Jesus Christ.* Christ is the supreme expression of the nature of God, "the exact representation of his being" (Heb. 1:3). No one has seen God except the Son; he who is at the Father's side "has made him known" (John 1:18). Knowledge of God is mediated by the Son. Praise to God returns along the same route. Barclay notes that the motto of the Benedictine order is, "In order that in all things God may be glorified."

The *NIV* understands the final sentence of the paragraph as a doxology: *To him be the glory and the power for ever and ever.* A comparison of the Greek text of 1 Peter 5:11 and 2 Peter 3:18 (both are standard doxologies) indicates that the present verse is a declaration rather than a doxology ("Glory and strength belong to Christ for ever and ever"). Those who think it strange that such qualities be ascribed to Christ rather than God (many commentators refer this "doxology" to God) overlook the unambiguous reference in 2 Peter 3:18 of eternal glory to the Son.

The addition of *Amen* marks the previous phrases as liturgical. It is a way of responding affirmatively to the truth just expressed.

A THEOLOGY OF SUFFERING (4:12-19)

12 Peter addresses his brothers and sisters in the faith as *Dear friends.* A stronger translation is necessary in order to convey the rich meaning of the Greek term. *Agapētos* describes Christ's relationship to God in Matthew 3:17 ("This is my Son, the beloved one"). It is used of the close relationship between Paul and Timothy (1 Cor. 4:17). The Christians at Rome are the "beloved of God" (Rom. 1:7). The "beloved ones" to whom Peter writes have been so transformed by the love of God that they now live in a loving relationship with one another. Persecution had come. Those beginning to suffer needed to remember that they were members of a fellowship knit together by mutual concern and affection.

Verses 12 and 13 tell us several things about the believer and persecution. First, the "trial by fire" through which they were passing should not take them aback. *Do not be surprised at the painful trial you are suffering.* Gentile Christians would be less apt to expect religious persecution than would their Jewish friends. The Jews had a long history of active opposition. They knew what it meant to suffer for one's religious beliefs. This, however, would be a somewhat new experience for Gentiles who had enjoyed the tolerance extended to local religions that in no way offended the authorities. The unexpected nature of these trials is emphasized by the clause *as though something strange were happening to you.*

The high standards of Christianity made society uneasy. By aspiring to the teaching of Christ believers had inadvertently become the conscience of society. Mankind has always been troubled by its conscience, and persecution has been the normal response.

The church should be accustomed to persecution. Early in the public ministry of Jesus he spoke of reproach, persecution, and unjust accusations (Matt. 5:11). John, sounding remarkably like Peter, writes, "Do not be surprised, my brothers, if the world hates you" (1 John 3:13). The lack of opposition to the twentieth-century church should be a matter of concern. Has the secular world grown more tolerant of religious people or have we failed to take the claims of Christ with sufficient seriousness? Has the church become little more than a country club with a steeple? Each local congregation should ponder these questions.

"Painful trial" translates a Greek word that means literally "the process of burning." Figuratively it refers to the purifying of metal by fire. The "fiery ordeal" (Weymouth) through which they were passing had as its purpose the refining of their faith. This brings us to the second insight concerning persecution and the believer—it comes in order to test the reality of our Christian commitment. It proves our dedication in that it provides the opportunity to demonstrate our fidelity to Christ in the face of opposition. Persecution reveals those whose faith is genuine. Fire separates gold from dross. Trial separates true believers from those who for whatever reason pretend to believe.

13 A third truth is that believers are to rejoice (rather than be taken by surprise) when persecution comes. The kind of persecution Peter talks about stems from allegiance to Christ and the church. Rejoice insofar as (or, in the degree that) _you participate in the sufferings of Christ._ The idea of sharing in the sufferings of Christ recurs throughout the New Testament (e.g., Rom. 8:17; Phil. 3:10; 2 Tim. 2:12). While obviously we do not share in the actual suffering of Christ (his death for sin), we do have a part in the suffering that results from living out in a hostile world the implications of his death.

Believers share now in the sufferings of Christ _so that [they] may be overjoyed when his glory is revealed._ Goodspeed uses the expression "triumphantly happy." God's way to joy leads through sorrow. Yet this sorrow is permeated with the joy of what will be. Jesus is the One "who for the joy set before him endured the cross" (Heb. 12:2). As the Pioneer and Perfecter of our faith, he leads us out on the path we are to take. The day of eternal rejoicing awaits the faithful pilgrim. Yet even now, although the path leads through an alien and hostile land, the journey calls for joy.

It is important to note that the day of revelation will be a time when the glory of God will be fully manifested. The root meaning of "glory" is brightness, splendor, radiance.

Christ described his heavenly state as having entered into "his glory" (Luke 24:26). When he returns at the end of time, it will be with a full disclosure of divine splendor. At that time the faithful will rejoice with exceeding joy.

14 From the very beginning the Christian faith has been marked by paradoxes. The beatitudes of the Sermon on the Mount jarred the sensitivities of those who felt that religion was primarily intended to help people adjust to the realities of life. Not so, said Jesus. The blessed are not the self-confident and aggressive but the poor in spirit and those who mourn. The ideals and social values of man apart from Christ must give way to an entirely different set of standards. The kingdom of God is a radical invasion into the territory of conventional assumptions.

In the character and spirit of his master Peter writes, *If you are insulted because of the name of Christ, you are blessed* (see Matt. 5:11-12). To "insult" means to reproach or revile. The word is used of the mocking of Jesus on the cross (Mark 15:32). In the Greek Old Testament it describes the reproaches heaped upon God and his people by the wicked (Pss. 35:7; 73:10). When believers are the object of scorn and abuse, they must realize that in that very circumstance they are blessed. They are to count themselves fortunate. Why? Because *the spirit of glory and of God rests upon [them].* The Greek text is unclear and has led to several interpretations of this clause. Some hold that the glory is a personal reference to the Son. Others take it to mean the Shekinah glory, that luminous glow of the presence of God which led the Israelites in the wilderness and dwelt in the tabernacle. As Stephen at his stoning saw the heavens open and the glory of God (Acts 7:55-60), so subsequent martyrs are blessed by the manifestation of divine glory.

It is probable that the expression should be taken as a single unit and translated "the glorious Spirit of God" (Goodspeed). To suffer for Christ is to be blessed because God's glorious Spirit comes to rest upon all who endure reproach for him.

15 Peter now adds a qualification so no one will misunderstand what he is saying. *If you suffer, it should not be as a murderer or thief or any other kind of criminal.* This goes without saying. The penalty they receive for their antisocial activity is well deserved. It has no moral virtue whatsoever. To the first three terms that denote that which is punishable by law Peter adds another—*meddler*, a compound word occurring only here in the New Testament and probably denoting a busybody who interferes in the affairs of others. On one occasion it is used of a certain bishop who had gotten himself mixed up in the affairs of another bishop's territory. The person who makes it a habit to pry into the affairs of others is a prime candidate for suffering. The "Spirit and glory of God" by no means rest on that sort of person.

16 *If*, on the other hand, *you suffer as a Christian*, that is, for living a life characterized by those graces which flow from the Christ-like life, *do not be ashamed.* Opposition to your manner of life has no bearing upon its worth. The world has always lashed out at goodness. The crucifixion of Christ is the ultimate statement about the moral perversion of man. So, don't be ashamed if you suffer as a Christian. The very name, Christian, was originally a term of derision. It surfaced in Antioch (Acts 11:26) and was known to Agrippa, who with sarcasm remarked to Paul, "At this rate . . . it won't be long before you believe you have made a Christian of me!" (Moffatt).

Don't be ashamed of suffering as a Christian but rather *praise God that you bear that name.* Although unacceptable to those who persecute you, the name Christian is worthy of your praise. To hide or obscure what one claims to believe is a serious matter in an age of conflicting loyalties. No one honors a traitor or coward. So praise God that your life is sufficiently different from the world that they take the trouble to persecute you.

17 The persecuted Christian is to praise God because present suffering marks the beginning of the final judgment. *It is time for judgment to begin.* The "appointed season" has arrived and judgment begins *with the family of God.* The concept of a preparatory judgment is found in the pro-

phetic teaching of the Old Testament. Malachi tells of a messenger who will prepare the way. Like a refiner's fire he will purify the sons of Levi. He will "draw near to [them] for judgment" and be a "swift witness" against the wicked (Mal. 3:1-6; see also Jer. 25:29; Ezek. 9:6). In the New Testament this period is called the "beginning of birth pains" (Mark 13:8-13). It is a "judgment" that falls on the great family of God. Note that this "purgatorial cleansing" is taking place right now in this life as the believer lives out his days in the hostile setting of a godless society. It is not reserved for some intermediate period between death and entrance into heaven.

But why should the believer praise God for adversity? Because to escape suffering now places one in the company of those who will meet the righteous anger of God reserved for all who reject the truth. *If* judgment *begins with us*—and it has—*what will the outcome be for those who do not obey the gospel of God?* It is infinitely better to endure the wrath of man than the anger of God. If you suffer for righteousness' sake, think how terrible it would be to suffer for unrighteousness. God is never portrayed in Scripture as a sentimental being. His strong and virile love led him to sacrifice his most precious possession, his Son. Whoever disobeys this gospel must face the eternal retribution that accompanies the rejection of divine love. Note that Peter doesn't speak of "disbelieving" the gospel but of "disobeying" it. The gospel makes its demand on the will of man. It does not call for his opinion. The truth of the gospel is not at issue. People either reject the truth or obey the truth. They do not decide on its truthfulness.

18 This verse reflects Proverbs 11:31 as it appears in the Septuagint (the Greek version of the Hebrew Old Testament). It is quoted here in support of the point just made. *If it is hard for the righteous to be saved, what will become of the ungodly and the sinner?* It is hard for the righteous to be saved in the sense that leading a righteous life opens a person to all sorts of opposition and abuse. That this truth falls strange upon our modern ears reveals more about our commitment to Christ than it does about any current tolerance on the part of the wicked. There is little doubt that should Jesus have lived in the twentieth century his reception by mankind would have been any different. His opponents would have ended his career just as decisively, perhaps not by crucifixion but by some other, equally effective method.

His opponents would have ended his career just as decisively.

19 *So then*—and here is the conclusion—*those who suffer according to God's will* should do two things: they should (1) *commit themselves to their faithful Creator* and (2) *continue to do good.* The NIV, like several other translations, omits the Greek *kai* (and, even, also), which modifies either the subject or the verb of the main clause. In the first case it would indicate that not only those who are exempt from suffering are to commit themselves to God but also those who do suffer according to his will. In the second case it would mean that those who suffer should not only praise God but should commit their souls to him as well. Its position in the sentence suggests the former interpretation.

The Greek verb translated "should commit" is informative. In classical literature it was used of turning over money to a friend for safekeeping. There were no banks in ancient times, so a person leaving home for an extended period would want to place his coins in the custody of someone he could trust. To break such a trust was a serious offense. Sufferers may place their lives in God's hands with full assurance that he will guard the deposit with the greatest of care. The same verb is used of Jesus on the cross when he called out in a loud voice, "Father, into your hands I commit my spirit" (Luke 23:46).

God is the "faithful Creator." This term is not found elsewhere in the New Testament. The sense seems to be that the God who brought all things into being is completely capable of keeping inviolable what we commit to his care.

Committing oneself to God is not passive submission. It involves active well-doing. While believers will certainly endure the hostility of an unbelieving world, there is no place for a martyrdom mentality. Suffer in silence but get on with the job of living an active life of good deeds. Christians should be known for what they do, not for what they suffer. Fixation upon the difficulties of life robs the believer of the opportunity to display his concern for the welfare of others.

⑤

FIRST PETER FIVE

SOME FINAL EXHORTATIONS (5:1-11)

1 Because the church has been called upon to suffer in accordance with the will of God (4:19), it is therefore (the *NIV* omits the Greek transitional particle) necessary that those in charge of the local congregation carry out their responsibilities as shepherds—willingly, selflessly, and as examples to their flock. So Peter addresses this section of his letter *to the elders among you.* There is some question as to whether or not the following verses should be limited to the elders as the official leaders in the church or whether the term would include all older men (as it does in v. 5). That the Greek has no definite article ("the") favors the latter. In any case, the term refers to leadership within the church, and that responsibility normally belonged to the more stable and mature men in the congregation (see 1 Tim. 3:1-7).

The idea of eldership has a long and important history. At the time of the Exodus Moses appointed seventy elders to help shoulder the burden of leadership (Num. 11:16-30). From that time forward there were elders in the Jewish social structure. In the secular world elders gave leadership to their communities and were responsible for public affairs. It was therefore natural for the early church to set up an organization that placed in the hands of elders the responsibility for appropriate governance. On Paul's First Missionary Journey he retraced his steps through the towns he had evangelized and appointed elders (Acts 14:23).

Because of the tendency to read back into the New Testament developments that took place at a later date, note that in the first-century church the office of elder and bishop were the same. Acts 20:17 speaks of the "elders" from the Ephesian church who came to Miletus to see him. A few verses later (v. 28) they are called "overseers" (or "bishops"; see the note in the *NIV*). The word *elder* reflects their relative age, while "bishop" refers to their function as those who oversee (*episkopos*, from the verb "to look over"—compare the English "episcopal"). The more rigid distinctions between ecclesiastical titles belong to a later period of church development. The original flexibility allows us to understand the verses that follow in relation to leadership in the contemporary church.

In setting forth the obligations of elders Peter could have fallen back on his apostolic authority. But the Peter of the Gospels, so often aggressive and impetuous, presents himself in quite a different way.

He is, first of all, *a fellow elder*. The designation occurs only here in the New Testament. It emphasizes that Peter shares with them the task of caring for God's people. He understands the particular problems that vex them.

But Peter is also *a witness of Christ's sufferings*. Commentators debate whether witness means eyewitness or one who bears testimony. In Peter's case, it means both. He deserted Christ in the Garden of Gethsemane but later found himself in the courtyard of the high priest. There he saw the condemned Jesus being led away to be placed before Pilate (Luke 22:61-62). The time when "the Lord turned and looked straight at Peter" (v. 61) was for the overconfident yet well-intentioned disciple a moment he could never forget. He saw the suffering Christ, and consequently he could never escape the responsibility of proclaiming to others the meaning of that suffering.

Peter goes on to describe himself as *one who also will share in the glory to be revealed*. On the Mount of Transfiguration Peter and his companions saw the glorious splendor of Christ as he spoke with Moses and Elijah (Luke 9:28-36).

That this great event made an indelible impression on the
disciple is evident from his reference to it in 2 Peter 1:16-17.

In a fuller sense, however, the glory in which he shares
is a glory "about to be revealed" (Montgomery). Jesus had
promised the disciples that in the age to come when "the
Son of Man sits on his throne in heavenly glory" they also
would "sit on twelve thrones, judging the twelve tribes of
Israel" (Matt. 19:28). That glorious day is about to break.
Present suffering is already permeated with the glory of the
coming age.

2 Peter exhorts the elders to _be shepherds of God's
flock_. Three times the risen Lord had inquired of Peter's
love, and following each affirmation he had counseled "Feed
my lambs. . . . Take care of my sheep. . . . Feed my sheep"
(John 21:15-17). Peter could never forget that the major responsibility of the elder was to tend the flock of God. En-
larging the flock is the concern of every member. We are all
witnesses. But caring for the flock is the special ministry of
the elders. The verb "to shepherd" includes more than providing food. It extends to everything required for the safety
and well-being of the sheep.

The imagery of God's people as a flock of sheep is deeply
rooted in the Old Testament. Psalm 23 comes immediately
to mind. The Lord is our shepherd, and we are the sheep
who lie down in green pastures and are led beside still waters.
(See also Isa. 40:11; Jer. 23:1-4.) Although the flock belongs
to God, it is _under [the] care_ of the elders. Their role as
undershepherds is brought out in verse 4.

We now encounter three carefully chosen contrasts that
describe how the elders are to carry out their shepherding
responsibilities. Each pair consists of a negative statement
followed by a positive correction. They reveal a profound
understanding of the weaknesses that often accompany
leadership.

In the first place, the elders are to serve _as overseers_
(this phrase is omitted in some Greek manuscripts)—_not
because [they] must, but because [they] are willing_. The
first clause involves compulsion, although not as a result of

outward force. There exist a number of pressures that might
coerce a person into church leadership against his will. The
expectations of others, for example, have often put a person
in a position against his own best judgment. An overseer is
to carry out his pastoral responsibilities voluntarily. The
added clause, *as God wants you to be*, translates literally,
"according to God." The idea is that it is in accordance with
the will and purpose of God that you do what you do willingly. God neither compels us into his kingdom nor forces
us against our will to do a specific task. He draws us by his
grace. He invites us to respond to the ethical implications of
our new relationship to God. God is a gentleman. He wants
his children willingly and enthusiastically to love and serve
one another.

The second antithesis is *not greedy for money, but eager to serve*. The elders apparently received from the congregation some small remuneration for their work. Paul told
Timothy that elders who discharged their responsibilities
well should be "reckoned worthy of a double stipend" (1 Tim.
5:17, *NEB*). What Peter is saying is that elders should serve
not for what they may get out of it, but eagerly for the good
they can do. The love of money disqualifies a person from
leadership in the congregation (1 Tim. 3:3, 8; Tit. 1:7, 11).
The Greek term translated "filthy lucre" in the *AV* is a compound that carries the idea of gain gotten by disgraceful or
shameful methods. This concern for personal profit has no
place in the life of those called to serve the welfare of others.

3   The third antithesis points out that leaders are to
serve *not lording it over those entrusted to [them], but being
examples to the flock*. It is not uncommon for those in authority to lose touch with those they govern and act in a high-
handed manner. Arrogance is a professional hazard in leadership. That power corrupts is a truism being continually
demonstrated in the affairs of mankind. Jesus warned against
lording it over others, as did the rulers of the Gentiles (Mark
10:42). The path to greatness is to serve.

The *NIV*'s "those entrusted to you" translates an interesting Greek word that in the classical period referred to

"dice" or "that which was assigned by lot, e.g., an estate."
In the Greek Old Testament the word is used of an inheritance. Deuteronomy 9:29 speaks of the children of Israel as
God's inheritance. This suggests that those who fall under
the supervision of an elder may be considered as an inheritance. The elder relates to them in the same way that God
relates to his chosen people. Rather than domineering, the
leader is to be an example. He is to demonstrate in his conduct how to live worthy of the name Christian.

4 And now a word that is at once a timely reminder
and an encouragement to faithful stewardship. *When the
Chief Shepherd appears, you will receive the crown of glory.*
Leaders are reminded that they are under the authority of
Another. When he appears he will want to learn of those
whom he has committed to each undershepherd. At that time
he will also give to the faithful the crown of glory *that will
never fade away.* The Greek term comes from the name of
a flower (the amaranth) that legend says never fades or withers. It is therefore "everlasting." The "crown" is not the regal
diadem worn by royalty but the garland awarded to those
who won in the athletic contests. It denotes victory. It is not
so much a "glorious wreath" (Goodspeed) as it is a wreath
that consists of glory. Our crowning reward will be to share
in the disclosure of divine glory in the age to come. At that
time the faithful will stand with Christ in the victor's circle.
His glory will be our reward.

5 The first part of this verse raises several questions.
Who are the young men that Paul instructs to be submissive?
Are they simply adolescent males or does the term refer to
some subordinate office in the church, for instance, deacon?
In what sense can it be said that they should be submissive
"in the same way"? In the same way that elders are submissive in carrying out their pastoral duties (see 5:2-3)? Is it
permissible for the same word to designate a specific church
office in verses 1-4 and then be used broadly in the very next
verse to indicate men of advanced age?

All of these minor difficulties are solved if verse 5a is
considered as a detached fragment from an earlier section,

2:13–3:9. Believers are to submit to civil authority (2:13ff.), slaves to their masters (2:18ff.), wives *in the same way* to their husbands (3:1ff.), and husbands *in the same way* are to be considerate of their wives (3:7). It would be natural at this point to insert 5:5a, *Young men, in the same way be submissive to those who are older.* How the fragment became displaced (if it did) we have no way of knowing.

The point is that submission to those who are older (and presumably wiser) is socially appropriate for young men. In our day, when everyone wants to appear young, respect for age inevitably declines. The resulting social imbalance has upset the customs and traditions that constitute Western civilization. Cranfield remarks that the revolutionary spirit of the gospel that in the first century was turning the world upside down (Acts 17:6) was not a revolution in the interests of chaos and disorder. On the contrary it was "an attack on the established disorder of the world in the interests and in the strength of divine order" (p. 116). Respect for age and experience is still a social convention with lasting benefits. What is true of relationships within society at large is also true of relationships within the local congregation.

All believers are to *clothe [themselves] with humility toward one another.* The *NIV*'s failure to translate the Greek *pantes* ("everyone") leads the reader to assume that the second part of verse 5 is directed toward young men only. The instruction is for *all* believers. The verb is interesting. It comes from a word used of the apron that slaves wore to protect their clothing while at work. Peter would not have forgotten that moment in the Upper Room when Jesus rose from the table, wrapped a towel around his waist, and washed his disciples' feet (John 13:1-15). In the same way, believers are to "put on the apron of humility to serve one another" (Moffatt). Humility is not a feeling of worthlessness. It is that attitude which allows us to serve one another in ordinary and down-to-earth ways. Reflecting on his ministry in Ephesus, Paul could say that he had "served the Lord with great humility" (Acts 20:19).

But ethics must always have a theological base. Clothe

yourselves in humility *because "God opposes the proud but
gives grace to the humble."* To support his admonition Peter
draws upon a well-known saying (Prov. 3:34). The principle
expressed in this proverb occurs throughout the Old Testament. Psalm 18:27, for example, reads, "You save the humble
but bring low those whose eyes are haughty." Pride is the
original sin. Eve was tempted to eat of the forbidden fruit in
order to "be like God, knowing good and evil" (Gen. 3:5).
But God sets himself over against the haughty and the arrogant. He bestows his gracious favor on those who are humble. Jesus uses the same word of himself when he says, "I
am gentle and lowly-minded" (*TCNT*). Humility is recognizing the intrinsic worth of others. It is the candid appraisal
of others as the objects of divine love and therefore worthy
of one's sacrifice and service. Humility does not dwell on
one's own lowly estate or compare itself with others. It is
the decision to serve others on the basis of having been
served by Christ himself.

   6   From the quotation Peter now draws a practical lesson. Since God "gives grace to the humble," *humble yourselves, therefore, under God's mighty hand.* Selwyn translates
the imperative, "Allow yourselves to be humbled." In a context of affliction this would mean, Accept the difficulties that
bring you low. They have entered your life with the sovereign approval of God. You are under his mighty hand. This
last phrase is regularly used in the Old Testament in connection with the Exodus (Exod. 3:19; 6:1; 13:3, 9, 14, 16).
The sovereign hand of God not only redeems but also controls the process of spiritual education. If he has allowed you
to enter into a difficult place, remain there with meekness
to learn what it is that he knows you need to learn. Humble
yourself so *that he may lift you up in due time.* As Christ's
exaltation followed his time of humility, so he will restore
you at the appropriate time. Answer 26 of the Heidelberg
Catechism reads, "In [God] I trust, and doubt not . . . that
even all the troubles, which He sends to me in this vale of
tears, He will turn to my good."

   "In due time" probably means more than simply the

proper or fitting time. In the New Testament the term took on distinctly eschatological overtones. It came to indicate the last days, the time of the end (Luke 21:8; Rev. 1:3). Those who share now in the suffering of Christ will also share in the glory of the coming age. God will reverse the fortunes of men in the day of judgment.

`7 Most translations, unfortunately, begin verse 7 as a new sentence (*Cast all your anxiety on him*). This breaks the close connection with what precedes. The Greek text continues by means of a participle the sentence that began with verse 6. When we turn ourselves over to God in every situation of life, knowing that the One who led his people out of Egyptian slavery has allowed our affliction and is in full control, we are enabled to cast our anxieties on him. To recognize his hand in life's trials is to be freed from the anxiety they produce. Jesus encouraged his disciples not to worry about what they would eat or drink or what they would wear. God, who provides for the birds and adorns the landscape with flowers, knows what his children need, and he will supply. Man's responsibility is to seek God's kingdom and righteousness (Matt. 6:25-34). Peter's admonition is a summary statement of this section of Christ's great Sermon on the Mount.

Anxiety is out of place *because he cares for you*. The Greek term for anxiety comes from a root that means "to divide." Anxiety divides the attention and distracts. It prevents that calm repose of the inner man which should be the hallmark of the believer. Anxiety follows when we forget that God is the One who cares for us. We are not left adrift on the sea of chance facing shipwreck on the shoals of an impersonal destiny. We are under the care of a sovereign God who controls the course of history and is intricately involved in the everyday life of each of his children. Anxiety mirrors the fragile nature of our ability to trust. It decreases in exact proportion to our willingness to let go and trust God.

That God cares is the distinguishing feature of the Judeo-Christian tradition over against the other living religions of the world. The God of Christianity need not be coaxed or coerced into caring by sacrifice or acts of ritual obedience. He *already* cares. In his love he came and died for our sins even though we did not desire him. He is the father of the prodigal, waiting and watching for the return of the one he loves. Salvation consists in accepting that love, not in prompting it or deserving it.

8 To put away anxiety does not meant to lapse into inactivity. We continue to live in a world in which Satan does his best to trip up believers. So *be self-controlled and alert*. In both 1:13 and 4:7 the admonition to remain sober or be self-controlled has an eschatological setting. Believers are to maintain a mental and spiritual balance in the difficult days that precede the end. Satan is portrayed as an angry lion prowling about, looking for someone to devour. He is *your enemy the devil*. The first designation was used of an opponent in a lawsuit, and the second is the regular Greek translation of the Hebrew word for Satan. It means "the one who slanders." False accusation has always been a weapon in the arsenal of Satan. Deception is his *modus operandi*. Paul counsels the Ephesians to don the full armor of God in order to withstand "the cunning of the devil" (Knox).

Satan *prowls around like a roaring lion*. Some think that the imagery of the lion may have been taken from the cruelty of the arena. It would not be many years before Christians would be given over to lions in the "games" played out in arenas for the pleasure of the mobs. Figuratively, Satan is right now a prowling lion *looking for someone to devour*. He is aggressively hostile to the people of God. The word for "devour" means literally "to drink down." It pictures an animal swallowing or gulping down its prey (see Jon. 1:17).

9 Peter therefore urges, *Resist him, standing firm in the faith*. The danger facing the congregation scattered through Asia Minor was that persecution and suffering might cause some to deny their faith and fall away from Christ. "The faith" is both the Christian faith as a body of teaching and the personal trust of those who had committed themselves to it. In the difficult days that would usher in the end, it would be essential that Christians hold firm their confidence in Christ.

One motive for faithfulness is the knowledge that other Christians are facing the same difficulties. Stand firm *because you know that your brothers throughout the world are undergoing the same kind of sufferings.* What happens to one congregation is happening elsewhere as well. Persecution is the lot of all who remain faithful. To give up or withdraw is to fail our fellow believers elsewhere in the world.

10 Peter now sets forth a fourfold promise. God will *restore you and make you strong, firm and steadfast.* The *NIV* obscures slightly the fact that all four promises are set forth by separate and independent verbs. The first term (restore) is used in several contexts. In Mark 4:21 it is used of mending nets. In 1 Corinthians 1:10 it describes the joining together of members of a church in view of pending disunity. Outside the New Testament it appears as a surgical term for mending a broken bone and in a nautical context for repairing a damaged ship. It means to repair so as to place back into service. Suffering may take its toll, but God will restore. He will repair the "damage" and fit us for continued service.

The second term means to establish and make solid. The third means to fill with strength, and the fourth to establish on a firm foundation. The net effect of these four positive verbs is that God intends to restore and establish securely those who are now suffering on his behalf.

Note that it is God *himself* who will do this. God does not leave this restoration to secondary means. He himself is personally involved in the reestablishment of those who have suffered on his behalf.

God is described as the *God of all grace.* His unmerited favor is sufficient for any and every situation. It is available for every believer. Furthermore, he is the One who has *called you to his eternal glory in Christ.* The ultimate purpose of his call is that we might share in the eternal glory that is his. As Christ suffered and was raised to glory, so the faithful go through persecution en route to everlasting glory. The reward is eternal but is received *after you have suffered a little while* (see Rom. 8:18).

11 The section closes appropriately with a doxology: *To him be the power for ever and ever.* The attribute of power (Greek *kratos*) is used only of God in the New Testament. It is regularly found in doxologies and ascriptions of praise (see Jude 25; Rev. 1:6). The appropriate response is *Amen,* so let it be.

ONE LAST WORD (5:12-14)

12 Most writers hold that at this point Peter takes pen in hand and writes the last few sentences himself. It has been noted that the Greek of 1 Peter is quite elegant. This raises the problem of how a Galilean fisherman whose provincial accent was unmistakable (Luke 22:59) and who, according to Luke, was "illiterate" (Weymouth) and "without learning" (Acts 4:13, Knox) could write such polished prose. That problem is solved by Peter's statement, *with the help of Silas . . . I have written to you.* Silas (or Silvanus, as many translations read—Silas is the Greek form of an Aramaic name and Silvanus is a Latin name that sounds much the same) was a Roman citizen (Acts 16:36-37) and responsible not only for delivering the letter to Christian congregations throughout Asia Minor (1:1) but for its literary composition as well. The use of an amanuensis (a scribal assistant who was often permitted considerable liberty in putting a message into the proper literary form) was common in the ancient world. Silvanus is undoubtedly responsible for the excellent Greek style of 1 Peter.

An additional word needs to be said about Silas. We know him as a leader of the Jerusalem church who was sent to Antioch to deliver the important verdict of the Apostolic Council (Acts 15:22-23). He became Paul's colleague and traveling companion on the Second Missionary Journey (he is mentioned nine times in Acts 15:34-18:5). In 2 Corinthians 1:19 he is listed as a fellow preacher. Paul names him as the joint author of both 1 and 2 Thessalonians

(1 Thess. 1:1; 2 Thess. 1:1). These references indicate that Silas was an influential person in the early church. He was Paul's assistant and Peter's penman, yet his highest commendation is that he was *a faithful brother.* "Well done, good and faithful servant" is the ultimate commendation (Matt. 25:21). It determines whether man will share eternal happiness (vv. 21, 23) or suffer the torment of outer darkness (vv. 26-27, 30). Paul writes that "it is required that those who have been given a trust must prove faithful" (1 Cor. 4:2). Silas was such a man—content to take a subordinate place and faithfully carry out the responsibilities that fell to him. The church desperately needs men like Silas who will work quietly in the supportive roles of Christian ministry.

Peter notes that he has *written to [them] briefly,* a bit of a surprise in that his letter contains 105 verses. (The author of Hebrews, however, says the same thing at the close of a much longer letter; Heb. 13:22.) A letter of any length about such important matters would be short in comparison with what could be written or what the author would like to write. A disclaimer of this sort is common in social rhetoric.

Peter's twofold purpose in writing is stated as *encouraging you and testifying that this is the true grace of God.* The doctrinal base of his ministry is the fundamental truth of the saving grace of God in Christ Jesus. It is to this message that Peter bears testimony. But his ministry includes encouragement as well. The Christian message must be transformed into changed lives. The purpose of doctrine is less to instruct than it is to provide the theological basis for a new way of living. So Peter encourages as well as testifies. The two are inseparably intertwined throughout his letter.

Now that you know the true grace of God, *stand fast in it.* Like Silas, be faithful to that fundamental truth which has revolutionized your life. Versions that translate the verb as indicative ("wherein ye stand," *AV*) rather than imperative ("stand fast," *NIV*) follow an inferior manuscript tradition.

13 And now the final greeting. Peter sends regards from *she who is in Babylon* and from *my son Mark.* Some writers suggest that Peter is sending greetings from members of his own personal family. "She who is in Babylon" could be a reference to the apostle's wife (the word *church*, added by the *AV*, is not in the Greek text). We know from 1 Corinthians 9:5 that Peter's wife traveled with him in his ministry. Tradition says that Peter's wife was a well-known martyr of the Christian church. Clement of Alexandria (born about AD 150) records her execution, which was witnessed by Peter himself. It is far more probable, however, that the "she who is in Babylon" refers to the church in Rome. Revelation 17 and 18 refer repeatedly to Rome as "Babylon." She is the "mother of prostitutes" (17:5) whose adulterous practices have led the entire world astray. She is the world center of corruption and ungodliness. It is from Rome that Peter wrote.

The church at Rome is *chosen together with* the congregation in exile in Asia Minor. Their common relationship to the one Lord constitutes the basis for their relationship to one another.

Peter also sends the greetings of "[his] son Mark." The reference is undoubtedly to John Mark who wrote the second gospel. We know him as the young man who left with Paul and Barnabas on their First Missionary Journey but turned back upon landing on the mainland of Asia Minor (Acts 13:13; 15:36-41). According to Papias, a second-century bishop who collected a number of early traditions, Mark was "Peter's interpreter" and "wrote down accurately" what he remembered about Jesus' life and teaching. He was Peter's "son" in the same way that Timothy was a "son" of Paul (1 Tim. 1:2; 2 Tim. 1:2).

14 Fellow believers are to *greet one another with a kiss of love*. It was customary within Judaism for a disciple to kiss his rabbi on the cheek. The kiss of greeting was common in ancient cultures. Jesus rebuked Simon the Pharisee for not having given him the kiss of greeting (Luke 7:44-46). Judas turned the customary kiss into an act of treason (Mark 14:44-45). By the second century the kiss had become a regular feature of congregational worship. It may have come immediately before communion as an expression of Chris-

tian love and unity. The kiss that Peter refers to, however, was a normal greeting. Paul makes reference to it in such passages as Romans 16:16 and 1 Corinthians 16:20 (where Phillips aptly translates, "Shake hands all around").

The letter began with peace (1:2) and closes in the same way. *Peace to all of you who are in Christ.* Perhaps the aging disciple could still hear Jesus' final words in the Upper Room, "I have told you these things, so that in me you may have peace. In this world you will have trouble (and Peter writes to those in severe distress and persecution). But take heart! I have overcome the world" (John 16:33). Victory over suffering by quiet endurance is the message of 1 Peter. Little wonder that the epistle ends on the note of peace!

A COMMENTARY
ON
2 Peter

INTRODUCTION

Who was the author of the book we call 2 Peter? That is the major question dealt with in New Testament Introductions and technical commentaries. J.N.D. Kelly, a contemporary writer of considerable reputation, says, "Scarcely anyone nowadays doubts that 2 Peter is pseudonymous" (*A Commentary on the Epistles of Peter and of Jude*, p. 235)—that is, it was written at a later date and assigned to Peter. He continues, "We must therefore conclude that 2 Peter belongs to the luxuriant crop of pseudo-Petrine literature which sprang up around the memory of the Prince of the Apostles" (p. 236).

Before we ask why so many current scholars are convinced that Peter did *not* write the letter, let's see what the author has to say about himself. In the very first verse he identifies himself as "Simon Peter, a servant and apostle of Jesus Christ." Obviously he intends his readers to understand that he is Peter, one of the Twelve.

The letter contains a number of personal allusions that support the author's claim to be the apostle Peter. In 1:14 he refers to the post-resurrection word of Christ to him regarding the way he would die (see John 21:18-19). In the same chapter he recalls the Transfiguration and says on two occasions that he was an eyewitness (1:16, "we were eyewitnesses of his majesty"; 1:18, "we ourselves heard this voice that came from heaven when we were with him on the sacred mountain"). In 3:1 he claims to be writing a second letter to them (an obvious reference to 1 Peter), and in 3:15 he refers to Paul as a contemporary. Either the letter was in fact written by the apostle Peter or it must be a forgery of some sort.

Pseudonymity is a polite way of saying that the letter was written by someone other than Peter and then assigned to the apostle. No persuasive reason, however, has been advanced to explain why this letter should be taken as pseudepigraphic. It contains no unorthodox tendencies as do most pseudonymous writings. It doesn't touch upon any of the major second-century problems, such as gnosticism with its doctrine of angelic intermediaries and creation by a Demiurge. Furthermore, the evidence we have militates against the probability of a false writing being included in the canon. For instance, the *Gospel of Peter* was banned toward the end of the second century on the ground that it was not written by the author it claimed. The presbyter who wrote the *Acts of Paul and Thecla* was severely disciplined by the early church. We should not suppose that passing off a letter as having been written by an apostle was all that simple. The readers of that day were perceptive and not at all given to uncritical acceptance of literary works claiming apostolic authorship.

The arguments against Petrine authorship include the following: (1) extensive borrowing from Jude, (2) difference in style and vocabulary from 1 Peter, (3) anachronisms that betray a later period, and (4) doctrinal differences. Counterarguments have been raised: that Jude was written before 2 Peter is not established; stylistic variations would be expected if the author used two different amanuenses; anachronisms are often too subjective to be considered historically dependable evidence (especially in *ancient* literature); and so-called doctrinal differences more often than not turn out to be variations in emphasis resulting from the immediate needs of the congregation (e.g., believers in 1 Peter are threatened by persecution while in 2 Peter they are up against false doctrine).

It is the position of this commentary that 2 Peter was written by the apostle Peter. It was written in the mid-60's, probably from Rome, and sent to essentially the same congregations that had earlier received 1 Peter. Arguments against the Petrine authorship accurately point out stylistic differences but draw conclusions that go beyond the data.

⑥

SECOND PETER ONE

ANOTHER LETTER FROM PETER (1:1-2)

1 For many readers it will be unnecessary to affirm that the author of this second letter was Simon Peter the disciple of Jesus. A number of scholars, however, think that it was written by some second-century person who passed it off as an earlier letter by the apostle. The reasons are laid out in commentaries more critical than ours. The problems raised by technical scholarship are of less weight than the indisputable fact that the writer himself claims to be the apostle Peter.

In the first place, the letter begins with the formal introduction, *Simon Peter, a servant and apostle of Jesus Christ.* "Simon" is his personal name, and "Peter" is the name given to him by Jesus, who declared, "You are Simon, the son of John. You will be called Cephas (which, when translated, is Peter)" (John 1:42). The letter contains other claims to have been written by Peter. Later in Chapter 1 the writer speaks of his death, adding "as our Lord Jesus has made clear to me" (v. 14; see also John 21:18-19). Then, referring to the great transfiguration scene, he continues, "We were eyewitnesses of his majesty . . . when we were with him on the sacred mountain" (vv. 16-18; see also Luke 9:28-36). Again, in Chapter 3, "This is now my second letter to you"—which doesn't prove 1 Peter was the first, but the burden of proof lies on those who would deny it. So we hold that Peter, the "big fisherman" and disciple of Jesus, was the author of what we call 2 Peter.

The first letter dealt with difficulties from without. We learned how to suffer for doing good, even as Christ suffered (1 Pet. 3:17; 4:1, 16-19; 5:10). In fact, we actually "participate in the sufferings of Christ" (1 Pet. 4:13). Now, in this second letter, we will learn of difficulties from within the church. Chapter 2 and most of Chapter 3 deal with false teachers who surreptitiously bring in destructive heresies. One has to do with the return of Christ—which they smugly deny saying, "Where is this 'coming' he promised?" (2 Pet. 3:4). But more of that later. Let's return to the beginning of the letter.

Peter identifies himself in two important ways. First he is a "servant." The translation "slave" (Montgomery) is misleading. In the Greco-Roman world *doulos* (slave) connoted many of the ideas we normally connect with slavery (e.g., absolute obedience, no personal privileges or prerogatives). The Judeo-Christian tradition, however, throws a different light on the subject. *Doulos* was a title of honor. Moses was a "servant of the Lord" (Deut. 34:12), as were Joshua, David, Paul, and James. Both the prophets of the old dispensation (Amos 3:7) and those of the new (Acts 2:18) are called servants of God. While being a servant of God involves unquestioning obedience, the context is one of privilege rather than oppression.

Peter is also an "apostle of Jesus Christ." God chose him for a special task and sent him out with the authority and power to carry it out. He was God's duly appointed spokesman for the new age.

The letter is addressed to *those who . . . have received a faith as precious as ours.* Weymouth has, "a faith of equal privilege with ours." The term was used of people who, having moved to another country, had gained full citizenship. They enjoyed equal standing with those who were native to the region (compare Peter's defense of including Gentiles in the church on the basis that they, too, had received the same gift of the Holy Spirit; Acts 11:17). The contrast in Peter's letter is between the Gentile believers in the province of Asia and the Jewish apostles who took to them the Christian message. "Faith" here refers to the body of apostolic teaching. Later Peter speaks of the prophetic work from the past and "the command given by our Lord and Savior through your apostles" (3:2). Christian belief is not subjective response to a set of lofty ideals but acceptance of a body of doctrine that provides understanding of what God has done in history in order to restore fellowship with man.

The word *received* means to obtain by lot. It reminds us that our acceptance before God has nothing to do with our own efforts. We are his solely on the basis of an act of divine grace. While God is not capricious in what he does, neither is he in any way influenced by our imagined goodness.

We have received this faith *through the righteousness of our God and Savior Jesus Christ.* Note the exalted role assigned to Jesus. Not only is he the Christ (that is, the Messiah of Old Testament hopes and aspiration) but he is also both God and Savior. Some think that Peter here distinguishes two persons (reading the text "of our God and of the Savior"), but it is better to take the phrase in the light of Thomas' declaration to the risen Christ, "My Lord and my God" (John 20:28). In his Pentecost sermon Peter arrived at the same theological conclusion. By the resurrection and exaltation God had made Jesus "both Lord and Christ" (Acts 2:36). The deity of Jesus was not the invention of some unfortunate disciples who needed something to believe in, but the inescapable conclusion of an historic fact.

He is also our "Savior." He was named Jesus "because he will save his people from their sins" (Matt. 1:21). Although the designation Savior was not widely used of Jesus in the New Testament (perhaps to avoid comparison with the Roman emperors who often claimed the title), it does occur 15 times in the Pastoral Epistles (1 and 2 Timothy and Titus) and Peter. The faith received by the Gentiles to whom Peter writes placed them on an equal standing with the Jewish believers because God is absolutely fair and just. The *NEB* translates, "through the justice of our God and Savior." There are no second-class Christians due to ethnic or racial considerations. There is one gospel, one great family of God. His offer of forgiveness extends to all without preference.

2   Peter uses the same salutation as he did in his first letter (*Grace and peace be yours in abundance*), but he goes on to point out how it comes—*through the knowledge of God and of Jesus our Lord*.

Several points deserve comment. "Grace" is God's favor poured out on undeserving man. Peter had often been the recipient of the gracious activity of his Lord. Jesus had seen him fishing in the Sea of Galilee with Andrew his brother and graciously called him to another kind of fishing—fishing for men (Mark 1:16-17). When Peter stepped out of the boat to meet his master on the water, and, losing faith, began to sink, Jesus graciously reached out to save him from the waves (Matt. 14:31). After Peter cowered before the young maiden and denied his Lord, a young man at the empty tomb told the women to "tell his disciples and Peter" (Mark 16:7). Peter knew the healing power of divine grace. Grace, the divine source of all blessing, is coupled with peace, the deepest experience of the soul (Erdman). No greater wish could be made for the Asian believers who were to receive the letter.

The second part of the salutation shows how the blessings of grace and peace come to the Christian. It is through the full knowledge of God and of Jesus our Lord. The crucial word is knowledge. The usual word for knowledge is *gnōsis* (as in 1:5, 6; 3:18). Here (and elsewhere, 1:3, 8; 2:20) Peter uses the compound *epignōsis*, which stresses the completeness of the knowledge. Many writers point out that Peter's use of the term should be understood over against the Gnostic claim that they alone had access to the real and hidden knowledge. Peter says that the blessings of God rest upon those who know God personally and intimately through Jesus Christ his Son.

THE INEXPRESSIBLE JOY OF NEW LIFE (1:3-15)

3   Peter now expands on the idea of a personal knowledge of God and how it relates to the Christian life. The Greek text of verse 3 begins with a word translated "seeing that" (*ASV*) or "inasmuch as" (Moffatt) but omitted by the *NIV*.

Since "as" introduces a subordinate or secondary thought, we should perhaps add a main clause to read, "And I am confident that those blessings will be yours" *[since] his divine power has given us everything we need for life and godliness.* In the compact style of an introductory paragraph the omission of an obvious clause is relatively common.

The important thing is that God has given us everything we need for a life of genuine godliness. His provisions for the demands of living in a corrupt world (v. 4) are complete. They come to us from his "divine power." Since no greater power exists, his provisions are more than adequate for any trial that may arise. It should be noted that "has given" translates a Greek perfect participle. This emphasizes permanence. The gift *has been given.* We don't have to wait for some future empowerment. Provision has been made, and all we need to do is to lay hold of it.

"Everything we need" covers every contingency. But notice that it is everything we need "for life and godliness." God's provisions are spiritual in nature. While he normally meets our material needs, he always in every situation meets our spiritual needs. "Everything that makes for life and true religion" (*NEB*) is powerfully supplied by the One who wants to show to the world by means of his followers what it means to know God.

And how has he given us all things? *Through our knowledge of him who called us.* Christ is the One who calls us. It is through a full and personal knowledge (*epignōsis* again; see v. 2) of him that we receive the power to live a godly life. We have not been called to a task and denied the power to carry it through. God's demands are always accompanied by what it takes to complete the job.

The final phrase of verse 3, *by his own glory and goodness*, is usually connected with the preceding words and taken as the means by which Christ calls us. The glory and moral perfection of Christ are said to draw man away from his sin and toward a life of holiness. John, speaking for himself and his fellow disciples, exclaimed, "We have seen his glory, the glory of the one and only Son, who came from the

Father, full of grace and truth" (John 1:14). The moral excellence of Jesus Christ still draws man away from the shoddiness of sin. As in the case of the Prodigal Son, the memory of a better life and the hope of reconciliation continue to call us back to God. Sin is willful rebellion against what we know in our deepest self to be the right and honorable course of life.

4 It is not immediately clear how *through these*, that is, through "his own glory and goodness," *he has given us his very great and precious promises*. Some writers say that "these" refers back to "everything we need" (v. 3a), but this makes the sentence unnecessarily repetitive. It is better to take as antecedent the phrase "his own glory and goodness." As an expression of his glory and goodness he has given us his promises "great beyond all price" (*NEB*). These promises have been given once for all. There is absolutely no question but that they will be fulfilled. The promises referred to by Peter include such events as the second coming of Christ (1:16; 3:4, 9) and the new heaven and earth in which righteousness will be the order of the day (3:13). Evil men scoff at the idea of a "second coming" and ask rhetorically, "Where is this 'coming' he promised?," but believers know that any apparent "delay" stems from God's desire that men repent and not perish (3:9).

The promises have been given *so that through them you may participate in the divine nature*. This is an amazing claim. Peter says that by means of the promises given to us by God we are able to share his nature. In one sense this takes place when a person is born again. Paul says, "Christ in you, the hope of glory" (Col. 1:27). In another sense it points forward to that time when, after making our call and election sure by moral development (1:5-10), we are welcomed into the eternal kingdom of Christ (1:11).

It is often noted that in verses 3 and 4 Peter uses philosophical and religious terms that would catch the attention of any educated person in the Greek world. He speaks of "divine power," "godliness" (true religion), "goodness" (ethical virtue), "divine nature," and "escap[ing] the corruption in the world." All of these ideas were widely discussed in the religio-philosophical circles of the day. A basic problem in Greek thought was how to escape the material world and become like the gods. Dualism taught that matter was evil and spirit good. Salvation was escape from bondage to the material.

Peter, of course, was neither Stoic nor Platonist. Why did he use terms that could so easily be misunderstood? The answer in part is that Christianity necessarily shares the vocabulary of the secular world. But words have no eternally fixed meaning in and of themselves. Eugene Nida, renowned philologist and Bible translator, has said, "Words bleed their meaning from the context in which they are used." So Peter can speak of participating in the divine nature without compromising the Christian faith to contemporary philosophical thought. The Greeks believed that man shared the nature of the gods by virtue of being human. Not so Peter. Man could *become* a partaker of the divine nature but only by the grace of God. There is a world of difference between these two concepts. The first is humanistic and reflects the vaulted self-appraisal of natural man. The other is Christian and exalts the gracious provision of God for the reconciliation of man the rebel.

The second reason for having received the promises of God (according to the *NIV*) is that we may *escape the corruption in the world caused by evil desires*. This translation adds to what the original text actually says. "Escape" is not a verb, but an aorist participle—"having escaped." The verse says that having escaped the world's corruption we become (through the promises) sharers in the divine nature. How we escape corruption is a separate question, although this may be to some extent by means of the promises.

The New Testament views the world as hostile and corrupt. Paul says that Christ gave himself "to rescue us from the present evil age" (Gal. 1:3). John depicts "everything in the world" as "the cravings of sinful man, the lust of his eyes and his pride in possessions" (1 John 2:16). The world is filled with moral decay. Peter adds that this depravity and squalor comes from human passions (see Jas. 1:14-15). The burning desire to have and to control creates a climate of corruption. Salvation is not simply the assurance of eternal life but deliverance from the evil power of human greed and passion.

5 Peter is fully convinced that spiritual growth in the Christian life requires strenuous involvement by the believer. God has rescued us from a corrupt world and promised us a share in the divine nature. In fact, it is _for this very reason_ that we are now to commit ourselves to a life of moral and ethical growth. It may be that those to whom Peter writes were returning to false teachers because of dissatisfaction with orthodox Christianity. Their dissatisfaction, however, was in great part the result of their own lack of genuine involvement in spiritual growth. So Peter lays out a program of moral development consisting of eight virtues—beginning with faith and concluding with love. Such lists are common in the New Testament (e.g., 2 Cor. 6:6; Gal. 5:22; Col. 3:12-14; note the major role of love in each list). They remind us that being a Christian is not simply a matter of subscribing to a doctrinal statement. To be a Christian means to conduct one's life in a certain way. Partnership with Christ transforms the way people live, yet this transformation depends upon our full cooperation and personal involvement in the pursuit of high ethical goals.

Peter says, _make every effort to add to your faith goodness_. The verb is instructive. Originally it meant to provide the chorus (the simple verb is _chorēgein_) for plays given at important religious festivals. Drama is one of the major contributions of Greek culture, and the works of men like Sophocles and Euripides required large choirs. Citizens, usually prominent and wealthy, who underwrote the expense were called _chorēgoi_. Later the word came to be used more broadly to signify lavish giving. So Peter is saying, With all diligence generously add to your faith goodness. "Goodness" is the classic Greek term for virtue. Translators have taken it to mean "moral character" (Williams), "manliness" (Montgomery), "moral excellence" (_NASB_), "a noble character" (Weymouth).

To this goodness we are to add knowledge (in this context, unlike v. 2, probably practical knowledge). The arrangement of the eight virtues is rhetorical. They do not represent eight steps to be taken in that specific order. Like the Beatitudes of Matthew 5 they are various facets of mature Christian character. One writer has suggested that instead of reading "*to* your faith add goodness" we should translate "*by means of* your faith develop goodness." While the interpretation is acceptable, it goes beyond what the text intends.

6 To knowledge we are to add *self-control*. This term was central in the vocabulary of Greek ethics. It means mastery of the self, especially in terms of the demands of the senses. It contrasts with the undisciplined and animal-like lifestyle of the false teachers (see 2:12). Self-mastery is the goal of all ethical systems.

Next comes *perseverance*. The *AV*'s "patience" is perhaps too passive. The *NEB* has "fortitude," which brings in the idea of courage. Perseverance (which Chrysostom called the queen of virtues) is the willingness to accept whatever obstacles are placed in life's path and the courage to make them into stepping-stones. This virtue was especially important in view of the complaints of some that Christ had not yet returned (see 3:3-4).

7 *Godliness* is not only "devotion to God" (Phillips) but a sense of duty toward man as well. It is religion in the best sense—the kind of religion that James says looks after orphans and widows in distress, and stays clear of the polluting influence of the world (Jas. 1:27). *Brotherly kindness* is the spirit of affection that should characterize the relationship between the brethren in the believing community. But love for the brethren is not enough—there must also be *agapē*, love that is universal in scope, including all men everywhere. Jesus taught that by loving our enemies we show that we are sons of God, for God's love is not limited to those who respond (Matt. 5:43-48). Perfect love extends to all.

8 Verses 8 and 9 point out first in a positive and then in a negative way the results of having developed the eight virtues just listed. Those who *possess these qualities in increasing measure* will be kept *from being ineffective and unproductive in [their] knowledge of our Lord Jesus Christ*. In fact, the qualities themselves will keep the believer from being unfruitful. Moffatt translates the phrase positively— "they render you active and fruitful." Ethical living produces a spiritual harvest. Christians often desire fruit in their lives but fail to understand that it comes from a prior commitment to godly living. We are more apt to ask God to work *through* us than to work *in* us. We would like to change the world out there but resist any change where it really counts. Effective change follows the decision to use all our powers to become people of faith, goodness, knowledge, self-control, perseverance, godliness, brotherly kindness, and love (vv. 5-7).

To be active and fruitful we must constantly be growing in these eight virtues. The ethical life is a dynamic experience. One day's achievements will not take care of the next. Nor will one level of moral accomplishment serve from this point on. Ethical living calls for vigorous activity and constant growth.

Scholars debate whether the "knowledge" that Peter is writing about here should be taken as the goal of Christian living or be construed with the two adjectives ("ineffective and productive") in the sense of "in respect to." The first option links the phrase to the verb and reads, "They will bring you . . . into [or unto] the knowledge of our Lord Jesus Christ." While this is true, it is better in context to take the phrase in connection with the adjectives, "Neither useless or barren in respect to your knowledge of Christ." Verses 2 and 3 of Chapter 1 understand the knowledge of God as something the believer already possesses. Not to pursue actively the virtues just mentioned results in idleness and therefore fruitlessness as far as this knowledge is concerned. Our knowledge requires application and moral seriousness. This is what bears fruit. We are very much a part of the fruit-bearing process.

9 *But*, Peter continues, *if anyone does not have them* (i.e., the qualities listed), *he is nearsighted and blind.* The

Greek text reads, "He, being nearsighted, is blind." If the participle ("nearsighted") is causal, then it would be this nearsightedness that causes blindness. The word means "squinting the eyes." By shutting one's eyes to the truth learned when he turns to Christ, a person becomes spiritu- ·ally blind. It is a serious matter not to pursue the virtues that must accompany the profession of Christ. A failure at this point leads to spiritual blindness.

Some writers take the nearsightedness to mean seeing what is close at hand more clearly than what lies at a dis- tance. In this case the emphasis would be upon seeing those things which have immediate personal satisfaction while los- ing sight of that which lies in God's future. This, too, is a tendency of many Christians. The glories of Heaven fade because the present world absorbs all our attention. Those things are most real which we think about most. The world presses in and makes us forget that we belong primarily to an age yet to come. We are sojourners (1 Pet. 1:1) who merely pass through this life.

Not only is the static believer barren and blind but he *has forgotten*, as well, *that he has been cleansed from his past sins*. It is all too easy to lose sight of what God has done for us on the cross. The Laodicean church was marked by a blindness to past blessings. Christ counseled them to buy salve for their eyes so they could see. They did not know that they were "wretched, pitiful, poor, blind and naked" (Rev. 3:17-18). To remember our cleansing is to continue to be grateful for our forgiveness. In this section Peter is not only giving good advice to the faithful but anticipating his denunciation of the false teachers (Chapter 2). They were vivid examples of barrenness and blindness.

10 *Therefore*—in view of the encouragement and warning of verses 8 and 9—*my brothers, be all the more eager to make your calling and election sure*. This verse has always been a bit awkward for those who stress God's sov- ereign action in man's salvation. If man is passive and does nothing but exercise faith (and many hold that faith itself is a gift of God that man cannot resist), how then can Peter talk about making our calling and election sure, as if we had some say in our salvation?

To be sure, God does call and elect. He alone decrees who is to enter the company of the redeemed. But it does not follow that there remains nothing for us to do. Peter specifically says that we are to "put God's Call and Selection of [us] beyond all doubt" (*TCNT*). To be called into the family of God means to enter a lifelong transition from what we were by nature to what we were intended to be by God. We have a part in this. A significant part! We are to be "all the more eager" to respond to his grace in a way that is morally appropriate. We are to "make every effort" (v. 5) to develop a moral character consistent with our calling. There is no hint in the text that we are to do this unaided by the Holy Spirit. Salvation by works is not the issue. What is called for is ethical determination to live the Christian life in such a way that our election to such an honored place is made absolutely certain.

Two things follow: in the first place, *if you do these things, you will never fall.* This does not mean you will never sin. John clearly teaches that "If we claim to be without sin, we deceive ourselves and the truth is not in us" (1 John 1:8). What it means is that in the long march to heaven we will never fall out of rank and be left behind (this interpretation anticipates v. 11). The Greek negative is emphatic. It means something like "never ever at any time." By developing the moral traits of verses 5-7 we guarantee our safety on the road to Heaven.

11 Secondly, we *will receive a rich welcome into the eternal kingdom of our Lord and Savior Jesus Christ.* Believers who are serious about moral development not only walk life's journey without lingering along the wayside but upon arriving at its goal—the eternal kingdom of Christ— are provided a lavish entrance. The verb in verse 11 is the same as in verse 5. Here is a lesson that needs to be learned. As we add goodness to faith, knowledge to goodness, etc., we will receive a "rich welcome" into Christ's eternal kingdom.

Christ's kingdom is eternal not only because it is without end (see Luke 1:33) but also because it is the kingdom of the Eternal One. The emphasis is qualitative more than temporal. Eternity will not be endless sequence as much as it will be the presence of the One in whom time ceases to have significance. He is before, during, and after all things. To enter his kingdom is to share in this perspective.

For the title "our Lord and Savior Jesus Christ" compare verse 1 where the only difference is "God" rather than "Lord." The meaning is the same.

12 Making one's election sure and gaining a rich welcome into the eternal kingdom is of surpassing importance. *So*, says Peter, *I will always remind you of these things*. The need for Christian virtue and the danger of what happens when a believer fails to pursue God's plan for ethical growth cause the apostle to remind his readers again and again of all he has been sharing with them. Unlike the false teachers who deal in "empty, boastful words" that appeal to the desires of the sinful human nature (2:18), Peter is content to dwell on the truth that has already been given. The Christian faith is not a heady search for new truth, but allegiance to the truth regarding Jesus Christ and what his death and resurrection imply. Jesus Christ is God's supreme self-revelation (John 1:18; Col. 1:15; Heb. 1:1). Who he is and what he did is at the heart of all knowledge. All subsequent revealed truth looks back to its source in Christ. This does not imply that contemporary Christians should be cultural ignoramuses. It means rather that what we are now learning is to be judged in terms of what God has already revealed. There is a need for informed believers who will stand at the boundary between scriptural truth and contemporary thought. What they need to remember, however, is that God's primary revelation took place 2,000 years ago. It stands as the measure by which we judge all later truth.

Peter continues to remind his readers of the basic truths of the Christian faith *even though [they] know them and are firmly established in the truth [they] now have*. The church is firmly grounded in the truth "that has already reached

[them]" (*NEB*). The Greek text says, "the present truth." To be well established in truth means not only to understand what it says but also to grasp its implications for daily conduct. For instance, many people understand that the death of Christ was a sacrifice for sin. Fewer grasp the fact that this death is also the believer's death: that from this point forward he is freed from the dominion of sin and enabled to live unto righteousness. Fortunately, Peter can say that his Christian colleagues scattered aboard (1 Pet. 1:1) are securely established in such truth. Yet he reminds them of it. Why? Because there are some things you can't know too well.

13 *I think it is right to refresh your memory as long as I live in the tent of this body.* Repetition was the major method of teaching in antiquity. When only a few individuals could write and paper (basically papyrus in those days) and ink were scarce, learning was done largely by rote. Stories abound of the incredible memories of ancient sages. Repetition played the major role in fixing information in the mind. We moderns who rely so much on notes miss much of the blessing of carrying in our memories the truths of Scripture. Christian organizations such as the Navigators have realized this and planned a program of Scripture memorization with the aim of fixing indelibly in the believer's mind the essential truth of the faith.

The image of the body as a tent is interesting. Some writers see a reference to the Greek idea of an immortal soul dwelling temporarily in a mortal body. For the ancient Gnostics this was held to be an unfortunate situation, but one that could be overcome by acquiring certain secret truths. The proper background for Peter's imagery, however, is the nomadic life of the Old Testament patriarchs. God dwelt in tent or tabernacle and guided the children of Israel from Egypt through the wilderness and into the promised land. The life of the believer is also nomadic. We are on a journey from earth to Heaven. Bunyan's *Pilgrim's Progress* is the classic allegory on this theme. Our destination lies ahead. We are currently camping along the trail. The body is a tent (a temporary dwelling place) that we use until the close of our earthly life. Paul speaks of an "earthly tent we live in" until it is destroyed, after which we will have "an eternal house in heaven, not built by human hands" (2 Cor. 5:1).

14 While Peter is still in the tent of his body he refreshes the memory of believers *because*, as he says, *I know that I will soon put it aside.* Peter is well along in years and knows that the end of his life is near. For this reason he seizes every opportunity to lay before his congregations the essential truths of Christian discipleship. The Greek word translated "soon" may also carry the idea of suddenness. From the following clause it appears that Peter is alluding to the violent death Jesus predicted for him. He adds, *as our Lord Jesus Christ has made clear to me.* In John 21:18 Jesus told Peter, "When you are old you will stretch out your hands, and someone else will . . . lead you where you do not want to go." Then John adds, "Jesus said this to indicate the kind of death by which Peter would glorify God" (v. 19). Tradition holds that Peter was crucified upside down. Since death was imminent, Peter uses every opportunity to reestablish for his readers the essentials of Christian faith and practice.

Note once again (see also 1:1, 2, 8, 11) the full title given to Jesus. The apostle loves to emphasize that Jesus of Nazareth was also Lord (sovereign ruler) and Christ (God's anointed redeemer).

15 Three times in this paragraph Peter uses the verb "to make every effort" (vv. 5, 10, 15). *And I will make every effort to see that after my departure you will always be able to remember these things.* Age had not lessened the zeal of Peter's concern for others. Even though his martyrdom was just around the corner, he continues to give himself without reserve for the benefit of those entrusted to his care. In fact, his approaching death furnishes the occasion for making provision for his readers after he is gone.

Commentators suggest several ways in which Peter may have gone about this. Some say that the apostle made provision for his congregations by setting up a succession of teachers. This obviously is conjecture only. Nothing in the

text supports the idea. Peter seems to be referring to some
sort of document that would serve the same purpose for them
as his own ministry. Thus, others have suggested that Peter
may have been referring to the Gospel of Mark. We know
from early sources that Mark wrote his gospel as a spokesman
for Peter. It might as well have been called the Gospel of
Peter through Mark. Irenaeus (a third-century church father)
understood the verse in this way. Many recent scholars think
that Peter is referring to the letter he was writing at the
moment. What he tells his Christian friends will serve to
remind them of the essentials of their faith whenever the
need may arise ("always").

The word translated "departure" is _exodos._ It is the same
word Luke uses in his presentation of the discussion on the
Mount of Transfiguration in which Moses and Elijah spoke
with Jesus about his "departure" (Luke 9:31). It means the
road or way (_hodos_) out (_ex_). It recalls the Old Testament
exodus—the "way out" of physical bondage into freedom.
In a real sense the death of every believer is the _way out_
from the restrictions of sin and mortality into the glorious
freedom of Christ's immediate presence. Death, for the
Christian, is not the end but the beginning. To cling to our
chains in fear of what lies beyond is to dishonor God. It is
an astounding lack of faith. To believe in him at all is to
believe everything he has promised. Our "exodus" is a glorious beginning, not a tragic ending.

PROPHETIC CERTAINTY (1:16-21)

16 A major purpose of 2 Peter is to provide believers with
certainty about the second coming of Christ. False teachers—"scoffers" is what Peter calls them (3:3)—had infiltrated the church, ridiculing the idea that Christ would return
in physical form. They argued that everything had continued
as it had always been since the dawn of creation. Thus, the
"coming" of which Christ spoke must have been of some
different sort. Peter says, _We_ (in contrast to the heretics) _did
not follow cleverly invented stories when we told you about_

the power and coming of our Lord Jesus Christ. The Greek word translated "stories" is *mythos;* from it we derive the English word *myth.* It appears regularly in the Pastoral Epistles (1 Tim. 1:4; 4:7; 2 Tim. 4:4; Tit. 1:14) where it refers to fables and legends about the gods. In Peter the "myths" are connected with the idea of a literal return of Christ. The false teachers had apparently allegorized what the apostles taught would be a real historical event and transformed it into a myth.

The line of argument taken by Peter is especially interesting. Usually in the New Testament the second coming of Christ is based on his resurrection (e.g., Acts 3:15-21). Since the grave could not hold him, it follows that he is who he claimed to be. Therefore his promise to return is absolutely trustworthy. Peter, however, bases the return of Christ on the Transfiguration, specifically on God's declaration on that occasion that Jesus was his Son and in him he was well pleased (Matt. 17:5; see also Mark 9:7; Luke 9:35). Along with James and John, Peter himself was there on that momentous occasion. So, "It was not on tales artfully spun that we relied" (*NEB*) when we told you about the power and coming of Christ, *but we were eyewitnesses of his majesty.* The word *eyewitness* was a technical term in the mystery religions. It was used of a person who had been fully initiated into the cult and allowed to watch its secret ritual. The word was also used in the ordinary sense of a spectator. This is how Peter uses it. The Transfiguration was an awe-inspiring display of the supernatural majesty of Christ. It was a foretaste of what will happen when he comes at the end of history to establish his reign. Since he has already appeared in the radiant splendor of his eternal state (the Transfiguration), there can be no question but that he will return in fulfillment of such a dramatic visual promise (the second coming).

17 Peter continues, *For he received honor and glory from God the Father when the voice came to him from the Majestic Glory.* "Honor" refers to the exalted position given at the Transfiguration, and "glory" to the radiance of his appearance (Matthew says his face shone like the sun and his clothes became as white as the light; 17:2). Translators have searched for just the right expression for the reverential paraphrase for the name of God. Moffatt speaks of "the sublime Glory." Others call it "divine" (*TCNT*), "magnificent" (Rotherham), or "wondrous" (Weymouth). Knox says, "the splendour which dazzles human eyes." Human language struggles without success to describe the greatness and majesty of the infinite God.

The voice coming out of the cloud (Luke 9:34-35) said, *"This is my Son, whom I love; with him I am well pleased."* Peter was there and heard God speak. About a week earlier Jesus had asked his disciples, "Who do you say I am?" In a moment of insight and faith Peter answered, "The Christ of God" (Luke 9:20). Now God himself reinforces that confidence by declaring Christ to be his Son. Not only his Son, but his Son whom he loves and with whom he is well pleased. While we know little or nothing about the inner relationships of the Trinity, we do know that Christ was obedient to the Father and that this brought great joy to the Father's heart. Obviously we are dealing with anthropomorphism— that is, speaking of God as though he were man. But how else can one speak of God? In fact, is it not highly significant that the relationship of father and son is the one used in Scripture to portray to us what we do know about God and Christ. It supplies our best insight into the nature of the triune God. God is not a static being, unaffected by what goes on in the world he has created. He loves and he can be pleased. These "emotions" extend beyond the boundaries of the godhead. He loves us, his creatures, and is pleased (or saddened) by the quality of our lifes and conduct.

18 Peter underscores his role as eyewitness, saying, *We ourselves heard this voice that came from heaven when we were with him on the sacred mountain.* Phillips translates, "We actually heard that voice speaking from Heaven." There can be no doubt about its authenticity. And we (Peter, James, and John) were right there on the sacred mountain (the mountain was made sacred by the event) when it all happened.

19 The final paragraph in Chapter 1 has been taken in two different ways. Verse 19 is basic. The Transfiguration confirms the prophetic teaching of the Old Testament; therefore, pay attention to it. Now for the difference: (1) the prophetic word is certain because it did not originate with man but on the contrary men were carried along by the Holy Spirit and spoke the words of God; (2) the prophetic word is certain but it is not to be interpreted by anyone on his own; it came from God through chosen men who were under the influence of God's Spirit (therefore, the apostles, not the false teachers, are the proper interpreters of Scripture). The choice is difficult, but we will follow the second approach.

And we have the word of the prophets made more certain. The majority take this to mean that the Transfiguration confirms the teaching of the prophets. An objection to this is sometimes raised on the basis that in the New Testament *events* are validated when they fulfill a prophecy, not the other way around (yet, see Rom. 15:8). It is the concurrence of prediction and fulfillment, however, that provides certainty. Each supports the other. Because there can be no doubt about the certainty of the prophetic word itself, other writers interpret the last words as indicating a greater degree of confidence on our part (as a result of the Transfiguration).

Now comes a note of warning, undoubtedly because the false teachers of Chapter 2 have twisted the meaning of Scripture to serve their own ends. *You will do well to pay attention to it.* It deserves careful attention. Since the prophetic word (a term that could indicate all or any part of the Old Testament) is in fact God himself speaking, it demands our undivided attention. The prophetic word is like *a light shining in a dark place.* The Greek word for "dark" carries the idea of squalid or grubby. It describes the world as it exists at the present time. It is an "evil age" (Gal. 1:3) marked by darkness and sin. The word of prophecy sheds light and provides guidance. "Your word," says the Psalmist, "is a lamp

to my feet and a light for my path" (Ps. 119:105; see also
Eph. 6:12; 1 John 2:8).

The Christian is to continue paying close attention to
the word *until the day dawns and the morning star rises in
your hearts.* The "day" is the day of Christ's return—that
glorious morn when the heavens shall open and Christ shall
return in victory to punish the wicked and reward his own
(2 Thess. 1:8-10). The "morning star" is Christ. The Greek
word (*phōsphoros*—compare our English equivalent "phos-
phorus") means "the one bringing light." Numbers 24:17
says of the coming Messiah, "A star will come out of Jacob."
In the last verses of the New Testament Jesus calls himself
"the bright Morning Star" (Rev. 22:16). As the morning star
heralds the dawn of day, so Christ anticipates the eternal
state in which there will be neither darkness "nor night (Rev.
21:25). Christ "arises in [our] hearts" in the sense that his
own resurrection portends that glorious day when we, too,
shall be changed to be like him. The anticipation rises in
our hearts.

20 Now comes an especially important point. *Above
all,* Peter writes, *you must understand that no prophecy of
Scripture came about by the prophet's own interpretation.*
The *NIV* follows the first of two options: namely, that prophecy is certain because it had its origin with God, not man.
The Greek has "no prophecy of Scripture becomes of its own
solution"—an ambiguous clause open to several interpretations. The majority of modern translators take a second option and refer the interpreting to those who hear it rather
than the one who spoke it in the first place. Goodspeed has,
"can be understood through one's own powers," and the
NASB, "is a matter of one's own interpretation." In view of
the context this latter approach is probably to be preferred.
The prophetic word was made certain by the Transfiguration,
but this word is not to be interpreted according to the whims
of anyone. This is what the false teachers were doing with
their allegorizing of the second coming.

21 Who, then, is qualified to interpret correctly the
prophetic word? The answer is indirect but given in verse 21.

For prophecy never had its origin in the will of man, but men spoke from God as they were carried along by the Holy Spirit. Prophecy is the result of God speaking through men moved by the Holy Spirit. Such men were the recognized leaders of the religious community. In the New Testament they were supremely the apostles. Peter is saying that the proper interpretation of the prophetic word is that supplied by the Spirit-inspired spokesmen of the New Testament church, not just anyone who decides to make of it whatever he wishes.

In addition to this basic truth, the verse tells us several important things about the nature of biblical inspiration. God's Word is *God's* word. He does not adopt and sanctify the best thoughts of man. Prophecy *never* had its origin in the will of man. No man can ever will a prophetic statement. It always comes from God. It is *his* word. Secondly, men who were chosen to be the channels for prophetic teaching "spoke from God." While the words they used belonged to their own vocabulary, what they said was a message from God. It was God speaking through them. And thirdly, "They were carried along by the Holy Spirit." It was the Spirit that enabled them to say exactly what God wanted them to say.

This, then, is the biblical doctrine of inspiration. The Bible we possess is God's word, his message to us. It came about when men moved along by the Spirit spoke God's message. Since God's utterances are always "living and active" (Heb. 4:12), the Bible comes to us today, not as a static record of Israel's religious history, but as a living word from an ever present God. Words on a page become a living declaration of the eternal God who now desires to lead us through the complexities of the twentieth century as much as he ever desired to lead the Israelites through the wilderness.

SECOND PETER TWO

HERETICS WILL NOT ESCAPE PUNISHMENT (2:1-10a)

1 Israel had its great prophets, such as Isaiah, Ezekiel, and Jeremiah, *but there were also false prophets among the people.* In Deuteronomy 18:20 God says that a false prophet is one "who presumes to speak in my name anything I have not commanded him to say." From the Old Testament we get a very unsavory picture of the false prophets. Jeremiah reports that they are callous toward the real needs of the people and are primarily interested in personal popularity (Jer. 6:14). Greedy for gain, they "tell fortunes for money," says Micah (3:11). They are "befuddled with wine," adds Isaiah, and "stagger when seeing visions" (Isa. 28:7). Worst of all, they lead people astray to worship other gods (Deut. 13:1-5).

As Israel had its false prophets, so also *there will be false teachers among you* (that is, the churches to whom Peter writes). Speaking of the last days, Jesus warned of "many false prophets" who would "appear and deceive many people" (Matt. 24:11). Writing to Timothy, Paul speaks of those in later times who "will abandon the faith and follow deceiving spirits and things taught by demons" (1 Tim. 4:1). Deceit has always been a major weapon in the devil's arsenal. He has mastered the art of twisting the truth to serve his own objectives. The end product bears some resemblance to the original truth—just enough to make it believable—but as it stands is rank heresy. As far back as the Garden of Eden Satan revealed his penchant for deceit and treachery. False prophets are his illegitimate sons and daughters.

Peter makes three statements about the false prophets. First, *they will secretly introduce destructive heresies.* The word *heresy* originally designated a philosophical school of thought. It was not necessarily false. Later, however, when Christianity presented itself as the truth, other points of view on religious matters were considered false, and therefore heretical. This was especially true of those subversive doctrines which claimed to be Christian. Note that the false teachers of which Peter speaks are said to have "cunningly introduce[d] fatal heresies" (Weymouth). Their methods were subtle and full of guile. As the word itself suggests, heresies are disruptive factions that bring about divisions among the people.

Secondly, the false brethren are guilty of *denying the sovereign Lord who bought them.* The concept of redemption at a price is central to New Testament theology. The Son of Man came "to give his life as a ransom for many" (Mark 10:45). "You were bought at a price," writes Paul (1 Cor. 6:20). The heretics were denying this basic truth. To be sure, they were not publicly proclaiming their unbelief. That would undermine their credibility with the very ones they wanted to lead astray. Rather, they denied *by their life* what they professed with their mouth. They did not "walk the talk." This is the kind of "denial" that is so devastating to the Christian faith. Those who openly repudiate Christ have clearly placed themselves outside the believing community. But those who say, "Yes, I believe," yet live out the opposite are the real deniers. Jesus said, "By their fruit you will recognize them" (Matt. 7:20). The way a person lives is still the only reliable indicator of his religious commitment.

Thirdly, the heretics are *bringing swift destruction on themselves.* Speaking of those who reject wisdom, God tells of a time "when calamity overtakes you like a storm, when disaster sweeps over you like a whirlwind" (Prov. 1:27). The day of reckoning will surely come, and with it sudden disaster for those who spread their pernicious doctrines in the name of Christianity.

Some have questioned why Peter uses the future tense in verses 1-10a. Are the heretics at work in other places and about to move into the circle of the churches to which he writes? Scholars who think that 2 Peter is a second-century epistle hold that the author used the future tense in order to convince his readers that it was written by Peter at a much earlier date. It is better to take the use of the future tense as a rhetorical device with no particular time reference. Beginning at verse 10b and continuing through the remainder of the chapter, Peter uses the present tense when speaking of the same false teachers.

2 False teachers and their heretical teachings bring about a twofold result. First, *many will follow their shameful ways.* For some strange reason deviant teaching always seems to enjoy a large following. The shameful or immoral ways of the teachers probably refers to their antinomian tendencies resulting from the false conclusion that since God's grace is unlimited they are free to sin all they want. For a definitive answer to this heretical position read Romans 6. Second, they *bring the way of truth into disrepute.* A favorite term for Christianity in its early stages was "the Way" (Acts 9:2; 19:9; etc.). It provided not only a goal for life but a way of living designed to take you there. The concept of two ways is set forth in the first Psalm—the "way of the righteous" and the "way of the wicked." One leads to life and the other to destruction. Jesus declared that he was the Way (John 14:6).

3 Peter goes on to describe both the motivation and the method of the pseudo-prophets. *In their greed,* he writes, *these teachers will exploit you.* The word for greed means "the desire to have more." The motivation for their "ministry" was not the welfare of others but personal covetousness. The object of their greed is not named. It could have been, as the *NEB* translates, a "greed for money," or perhaps, as others think, an overwhelming desire to take over the place of Christ himself. Christians were being used by the heretics for the sole advantage of the latter. This basic principle still prevails wherever social manipulators prey upon the weaknesses of people. For example, every modern ad that uses sex for economic advantage is guilty of the same cheap trick.

How did the false teachers carry out their program of self-advancement? By *stories they have made up*. The original says, by "molded words," that is, by words fabricated for the purpose of persuasion. They were words cunningly arranged to fit the situation and lead astray. Language was intended for human communication. It is a gift of God that has made civilization possible. Yet wicked man so often uses language to conceal and mislead rather than to communicate.

Peter notes, however, that *their condemnation has long been hanging over them, and their destruction has not been sleeping*. They stand under God's wrath. He has not overlooked their evil machinations. He will visit them with punishment. Sudden destruction will be their end (v. 1). A sovereign and just God will not let wickedness go unpunished.

This is an important point. God knows how to "hold the unrighteous for the day of judgment." This conclusion, found later in verse 9, follows three infamous examples of sin and the judgment to which each led. The angels fell and are in custody in Hell (v. 4). The ungodly world in the time of Noah was destroyed in the Flood (v. 5). Sodom and Gomorrah were reduced to ashes for their wickedness (v. 6). Thus God does not let evil go unpunished. Let the false teachers beware. Divine retribution is based upon the consistent action of a righteous God. Their evil has not escaped his attention.

4 Exhibit number one is the angels. *For if God did not spare the angels when they sinned, but sent them to hell.* The most common interpretation of this incident is that the angels were the "sons of God" (see Gen. 6:1-4) who cohabited with the "daughters of men" and produced the Nephilim (giants). The Hebrew text of Job 1:6; 2:1; 38:7 reads "sons of God," translated "angels" in the *NIV*. This particular legend is developed in the noncanonical *Book of Enoch*.

The more traditional interpretation understands it as a reference to the prehistoric fall of the angels who followed Satan in his rebellion against God. In either case sin is followed by judgment, and that is the point Peter wishes to establish.

The hell to which the fallen angels are consigned is neither *hades* (the place of departed spirits) or *gehenna* (the place of fire), but *tartarus*, a subterranean abyss reserved for rebellious gods and men. In Tartarus the angels who sinned are put *into gloomy dungeons to be held for judgment.* Their hour of decision has passed. Guarded in the dark caverns of the underworld they await their final doom. Note: The AV's "chains of darkness" comes from an alternate Greek textual tradition that reads *seirais* (chains) rather than *seirois* (pits).

5 Peter draws his second example from the wickedness in the days of Noah. *If he* (that is, God) *did not spare the ancient world when he brought the flood on its ungodly people.* Genesis 6:11 tells us that in that day "the earth was corrupt in God's sight and was full of violence." The only proper response to such extensive wickedness was for God to send a flood and wipe out the entire population. God is serious about sin. He does not let it go unpunished. If man insists on refusing the goodness of God and follows his own unrighteous paths, there remains no alternative for the moral ruler of the universe but to bring judgment.

Perhaps by way of encouragement Peter refers to the one exception: God *protected Noah, a preacher of righteousness, and seven others* (his wife, three sons and their wives; Gen. 7:13). The Old Testament tells us that Noah was a righteous and blameless man who walked with God (Gen. 6:9) but nothing about his preaching. It comes as no surprise, however, that Peter calls him a preacher of righteousness. Jewish legend held him up as an example of moral excellence. Preachers have long employed their most vivid imagination in describing Noah as he built the ark with one hand and waved the Bible with the other. So although the ancient world perished because of its corruption and sin, eight people were protected from the catastrophe because they were right with God. God's judgment, although certain and devastating, will never touch his own.

6 For a third illustration of God's intention to punish all wickedness Peter draws upon the dramatic destruction of Sodom and Gomorrah. *He condemned* these cities *by burning them to ashes.* The story is recounted in Genesis 19. The people of Sodom had demanded that Lot turn over to them for sexual purposes two angels who had come to warn him to flee from the city. Only by great persuasion were the angels able to convince him to leave with his wife and two daughters. God rained down burning sulphur on the two cities of the plain. When Lot's wife disobeyed and looked back, she became a pillar of salt. The story was well known to every Jewish family and its implications were perfectly clear. God will not tolerate wickedness. What happened to Sodom and Gomorrah has become *an example of what is going to happen to the ungodly.* Their judgment makes certain the judgment of all who live in like manner. Billy Graham is reported as saying that unless God brings judgment upon America he will have to apologize to Sodom and Gomorrah! Many practices tolerated in "Christian" America may well have been taboo in pagan Sodom. Unless America returns to a set of values far more Christian than she now embraces, judgment on a national scale is bound to come. The utter obliteration of two cities by fire from above stands as a warning that all others who pursue wickedness will come to the same fiery end. Small wonder that some are moved to placard our cities with signs that say "Repent, America, or Perish."

7 As God saved Noah (in the second example of divine judgment), so now he rescues *Lot, a righteous man, who was distressed by the filthy lives of lawless men.* That Lot is called a righteous man comes as a surprise to most. Wasn't he the one who offered his two unmarried daughters to the wicked men of Sodom who lusted after the visiting angels (Gen. 19:6-8)? And did he not succumb to the enticement of his own daughters and under the influence of wine commit

incest with each of them (Gen. 19:30-36)? How can Peter call him a righteous man?

8 To support his assertion Peter adds parenthetically, _for that righteous man, living among them day after day, was tormented by the lawless deeds he saw and heard._ There is no doubt that Lot was less than perfect. The biblical account makes that perfectly clear. But in a certain way he can be called righteous. That is, he continued to be distressed by the lewd conduct of the lawless society in which he lived. There remained hope for him because he had not abandoned in principle the righteous requirements of a holy God. He was still distressed by the open sinfulness of the people with whom he had so unwisely chosen to live. So God spared him. The message to the faithful in the churches of Asia is that although God's judgment is bound to fall on the wicked there remains a way out for those who cling to the standards of morality established by the New Testament church.

Newman is quoted as saying, "Our great security against sin lies in being shocked at it." Unfortunately sin loses much of its offense as it becomes commonplace in a society. The church should pray never to surrender its outrage against these practices which run counter to the will and nature of God. The fear of being labeled moralist has in many cases turned us into ethical chameleons whose only "virtue" is thoughtless tolerance.

9 Peter now draws his conclusion. It is based on the fall of the angels, the great flood, and the destruction of Sodom and Gomorrah. _If this is so_—and his readers would wholeheartedly agree—_then_ two things follow. First, _the Lord knows how to rescue godly men from trials._ It is significant that in a unit that starts with a forceful denunciation of heretics and a reminder of their sure condemnation, the summary begins with a reference to God's concern for righteous men. Both Noah and Lot were delivered while judgment fell on others. False teachers have infiltrated local churches and have deceived many into believing that since salvation is based upon God's grace it matters little how a person behaves. Believers are above the moral law, they

would argue. But God knows how, Peter asserts, to deliver the godly from all such trials as may be brought on by the intemperance and subtle sinfulness of false prophets who revel in unrighteousness. Don't be discouraged. God will see you through.

He also knows how to *hold the unrighteous for the day of judgment.* This is the final judgment of which Jesus spoke when he said, "It will be more tolerable for Sodom and Gomorrah on the day of judgment than for that town," that is, the town that does not receive the message of the Twelve (Matt. 10:15; see also 1 John 4:17). The unrighteous are under guard until the time the official sentence is enacted. The Greek text adds a single participle *(koladzomenous)* which the *NIV* translates *while continuing their punishment.* If this interpretation is right, then the wicked are being punished right now while awaiting final judgment and the destruction that follows. The *TCNT* has, "the wicked, who are even now suffering punishment, in readiness for the Day of Judgment" (see the account of the rich man and Lazarus in Luke 16:19-31). Some take the participle to mean that God is able to keep until the day of judgment *those who are to be punished.* Either is acceptable, but the latter seems to fit the context better.

10a Peter next identifies two categories of wicked men for whom certainty of judgment is *especially true*: first, *those who follow the corrupt desire of their sinful natures.* Peter has in mind the troublemakers of verses 1-3 (who are described in detail in verses 10b-22). They are pictured as ;~oing along with or being led by depraved desires. They have relinquished any semblance of morality and have abandoned themselves to sensuality. Paul talks of this kind of profligacy in Romans 1:21-32.

A growing segment of contemporary society claims that people are free to do whatever feels good or seems to be natural. What they fail to realize is that by nature man is a sinner. What he does "naturally" (meaning, led by one's own fallen nature) is bound to be wrong. Even thoughtful secularists understand that without restraint there can be no or-

dered civilization. Conduct without regard for others leads
to chaos. Add to this the theological insight that man's nature
has been corrupted by the Fall, and it is clear that a society
led by its animal impulses is a society destined to moral
holocaust.

The second category of those for whom God has reserved punishment are those who *despise authority*. They
are unwilling to live in an ordered society that places the
responsibility of civility and obedience upon its members.
The verses that follow suggest that the authority they scorn-
fully reject is that of Christ himself. They slander "celestial
beings" in the very presence of the Lord (vv. 10b-11). All
such conduct places them in line for judgment on the day
Christ returns. History has proven that God never overlooks
wickedness. Punishment is sure: the false teachers who were
stirring up the Asian churches with heretical and dissolute
lives will by no means escape God's attention.

PORTRAIT OF A FALSE PROPHET (2:10b-22)

10b-11 Peter now describes in detail the false teachers who
had infiltrated the Asian churches. Read the passage and
picture Peter the fiery orator telling his congregation in no
uncertain terms exactly what these people are like and what
lies in store for them. We are not dealing with a theological
temper tantrum by a religious fanatic but with a straightforward denunciation of error by a man of God who cares about
his people and is unwilling to see them led astray.

The heretics are *bold and arrogant*. Success in the tactics of deceit has made them daring and headstrong. They
are *not afraid to slander celestial beings*. While some hold
that reference is made to leaders of the church (Norlie has
"those in high repute"), it is clear that the object of their
scorn is angelic beings (Phillips calls them "the glories of
the unseen world"). Some commentators think that they are
the good angels through whom the glory of God shines, and
others, the angels who fell from their glorious standing before God. The latter suggestion rests on the following verse

which says, *yet even angels* (presumably the good angels who did not fall), *although they are stronger and more powerful* (than the false teachers), *do not bring slanderous accusations against such beings in the presence of the Lord.* The argument is that if the angels who did not sin withhold accusation against those who did, then there is no place for man (who is inferior in strength and power) to revile and insult the fallen angels. In the noncanonical book of 1 Enoch we have a picture of men complaining of the difficulties brought about by evil angels. An archangel lays the matter before God but offers no personal judgment. This sort of heavenly courtroom scene could provide the background for Peter's statement.

12 Contrariwise, *these men* (the pseudo-prophets) *blaspheme in matters they do not understand.* They sneer and scoff at things that are entirely beyond their competence to grasp. The most terrifying thing about ignorance is its inability to recognize its own condition. We all lack knowledge in certain areas. To be unaware of ignorance and act aggressively on matters of import is unfortunate in the extreme.

They are like brute beasts, Peter says, *creatures of instinct, born only to be caught and destroyed, and like beasts they too will perish.* The false teachers are like irrational animals. They are creatures of instinct. They have "no more sense than the unreasoning brute beasts which are born to be caught and killed" (Phillips). Although feigning great insight into religious and spiritual issues, they are totally without understanding. Like great dumb beasts whose lot is to be caught and killed, they too will perish. As they destroy others, they too shall be destroyed.

13 Peter continues, *they will be paid back with harm for the harm they have done.* The Greek text throughout this section is somewhat uncertain and is variously interpreted. The basic idea, however, is clear. The wrongdoers will be punished for the suffering they have inflicted on others. It is appropriate that injury and injustice should be repaid in

kind. Whatever a man sows, says Paul, is exactly what he
will reap (Gal. 6:7).

Find out what a man would most like to do and you will
know what sort of person he is. The false teachers' *idea of
pleasure is to carouse in broad daylight.* They are shameless
and vulgar in their pursuit of sensual stimulation. While as
a general rule men love darkness because their deeds are
evil (John 3:19), there is a level of degeneracy so low that it
delights in flaunting its immorality in full view of others.
They are blots and blemishes (note the contrast with Christ
the lamb of God who is "without blemish or defect,"
1 Pet. 1:19—the same two words negated), *reveling in their
pleasures while they feast with you.* For the word *apatais*
(AV, "deceivings"; the *NIV* has "pleasures" but the word
clearly has the idea of deception or trickery) some manuscripts read *agapais* (love feasts or agapes). This would indicate that the heretics had wormed their way into the very
heart of the Christian fellowship. They indulge in "wanton
revelry, even while joining you at your feasts" (*TCNT*). It
sounds very much like the lamentable condition at Corinth
where drunkenness and disregard for the needy were present at the Lord's Supper itself (1 Cor. 11:20-22).

14 *With eyes full of adultery, they never stop sinning.*
The word for "adultery" is actually "adulteress." Goodspeed
has, "They have eyes for nobody but adulterous women."
More probable is the suggestion that they find it impossible
to look at any woman without imagining themselves in bed
with her (Kelly). Their crude and promiscuous stare assumes
that every woman they see is a potential prostitute. *They
seduce the unstable.* Unstable believers are baited and trap-
ped by the false teachers. Cunning and deceit are their tools.
And now their motivation is revealed: *they are experts in
greed.* Their covetousness is so great that it would appear
that they have undergone special training (the verb has athletic connotations—*gymnadzō*, compare our "gymnasium")
in greed. *An accursed brood!*, contends Peter. "God's curse
is on them" (*NEB*).

15 *They have left the straight way and wandered off*

to follow the way of Balaam son of Beor. Scripture often describes conduct as a path to be followed. Psalm 1 compares the "way of the righteous" with the "way of the wicked." The straight (or "right," *AV*) way is the path of conduct laid out by God. The false teachers have deserted this way of life and followed the example of Balaam, the prophet of Israel *who loved the wages of wickedness* and, according to Revelation 2:14, "taught Balak to entice the Israelites to sin by eating food sacrificed to idols and by committing sexual immorality." (For the story of Balaam see Num. 22–24; 31:8, 16. Josh. 13:22 adds that he "practiced divination.") As Balaam "set his heart on dishonest gain" (Goodspeed), so these heretics were motivated by a greed that led them to deceive and exploit for personal profit.

16 Peter reminds his readers that Balaam continued to pursue the wrong course of action even though *he was rebuked for his wrongdoing by a donkey—a beast without speech—who spoke with a man's voice and restrained the prophet's madness.* Three times the donkey tried to prevent Balaam from going on: once by going off into a field, again by crushing the prophet's foot against a wall, and finally by lying down in the road. Upon being beaten by the prophet, the donkey spoke up and rebuked his master. The picture is one of a headstrong prophet so set upon going his own way that he has to be counseled, not by man, but by a beast of burden. Peter's antagonists are like the bullheaded prophet whose decision to follow the wrong course of action had passed the point of no return.

17 Peter continues, *These men are springs without water.* They promise refreshment but provide no thirst-quenching water for the spiritually thirsty. They are *mists driven by a storm.* Unlike rainfall, they lack any real substance. The example of the fallen angels who are held in "gloomy dungeons" (v. 4) is still in mind when Peter, using the same term, writes, *Blackest darkness is reserved for them.* They, too, will be cast into the dark regions of Tartarus along with the angels who rebelled against God.

18 The errorists carry out their program by a persuasive appeal to man's lower nature. They mouth *empty, boastful words.* "Arrogant nonsense" is Goodspeed's translation. Knox has, "fine phrases that have no meaning." Language—that God-given capacity to communicate and understand—has become for them an instrument to divide and spoil. Sin defiles everything it touches. It takes the very gifts of God and turns them into tools of iniquity.

It is *by appealing to the lustful desires of sinful human nature* that the heretics *entice people.* They bait their prey with an appeal to sensual desire and the prospect of no restraint (the *NIV* fails to translate *aselgeiais*, "excesses"). Much of modern advertising is nothing but a contemporary expression of the same principle. Everything from shaving cream to automobiles is sold through clever ads with sexual innuendoes. Twentieth-century man is duped in exactly the same way as his first-century brother.

The heretics exercise their deceptive practices on *people who are just escaping from those who live in error.* They prey on novices to Christianity—those who are not as yet established believers. Like hungry wolves they single out and attack the helpless. "Those who live in error" refers to the pagan population that has not yet come to the truth that is in Christ.

19 The heretics are especially fond of talking about freedom (which they hold out as the great goal of human existence) and bondage (the supreme calamity!). *They promise them* (those who swallow their line) *freedom, while they themselves are slaves of depravity.* It is a curious thing that those who are unable to break the chains of their own sinful habits should preach to others the virtues of unrestricted action. Sin is an intoxicating potion that befuddles the mind and makes impossible a rational appraisal of one's true condition. The false teachers argued that for a man to be free means that he is free to sin as much as he wants. They taught that believers were free from every demand of the moral law.

Not only were they wrong in their basic premise about freedom, but they were also wrong in regard to their own supposed freedom. So Peter quotes the oft-repeated saying—

a man is a slave to whatever has mastered him (see
Rom. 6:14). To be enslaved to one's lower instincts is not to
be free. Freedom is the power to do what is right. Only
Christ can set a person free (see John 8:36). Seneca (the Stoic
philosopher) is quoted as saying, "To be enslaved to oneself
is the heaviest of all servitudes." Yet natural man continues
unabated his quest for personal gratification. When it comes
to genuine freedom, secular humanism has nothing to offer
those who have committed themselves to Christ and his program for victory over self by concern for others.

20   The last three verses of Chapter 2 teach that it would
have been better for the false teachers never to have known
the way of righteousness than once having experienced the
cleansing power of Christ to return to their original corrupt
style of living. The text reads, *If they have escaped the corruption of the world* (and the Greek text assumes they have)
by knowing our Lord and Savior Jesus Christ (note Peter's
fondness for this complete title; see 1:1, 11; also 1:8, 14, 16)
*and are again entangled in it and overcome, they are worse
off at the end than they were at the beginning.* While this
is true in a special way of the false teachers, it is also true
of all who have been led to believe that faith in Christ places
a man beyond the restrictions of morality.

21   *It would have been better for them not to have
known the way of righteousness, than to have known it and
then to turn their backs on the sacred commandment that
was passed on to them.* It is better never to have known the
truth than having been exposed to it to have disobeyed its
basic moral teaching. Privilege involves responsibility. No
truth is better than truth refused or neglected. Jesus taught
that a servant who knows his master's will and disobeys will
be punished more severely than one who does not know—
"From everyone who has been given much, much will be
demanded" (Luke 12:47-48). The early church viewed apos-
tasy with great concern (see Heb. 6:4-6). For the one who
knows the truth there is no sacrifice able to cover his willful
decision to continue in error (Heb. 10:26).

22   Peter clinches his argument with two proverbs. He

writes, *Of them the proverbs are true*, that is, what they say
has already taken place. *A dog returns to its vomit.* The dog
was an unclean animal in that it ate whatever it could find
without regard for ceremonial laws of cleanliness. Jews,
therefore, regarded Gentiles as "dogs" (see Matt. 15:26). As
a dog returns to his vomit, so the false teachers return to the
impurity and corruptness of their lives before they claimed
to know Christ.

The first proverb came out of the Old Testament (Prov.
26:11). The second has no biblical background. It was undoubtedly current among the Greeks to whom Peter writes.
*A sow that is washed goes back to her wallowing in the
mud.* A pig's heart is not changed by washing its body. A
man's actions reveals what he is really like. The false teachers had been bathed—they joined the Christian flock—but
now they are back wallowing in the moral squalor of paganism. All of which proves that they are still "pigs" at heart.

⑧

SECOND PETER THREE

SCOFFERS AND THE LAST DAYS (3:1-10)

1 After a lengthy exposé of the false teachers who were upsetting the faith of new converts in the Asian churches, Peter returns to his basic theme—the coming "day of the Lord." His purpose is ethical rather than theological. He reproves the scoffers who misrepresent God's purpose in delaying the return of Christ. He explains that the world will ultimately be destroyed by fire, and that this knowledge should encourage Christian growth and character.

Dear friends, he begins, *this is now my second letter to you.* The former letter was 1 Peter, although for various reasons some have suggested a different letter that is lost to us. Some suggest the first two chapters of 2 Peter. Speculations of this sort stem from a reluctance to accept at face value the apostolic authorship of the letter.

Peter continues, *I have written both of them as reminders to stimulate you to wholesome thinking.* The last phrase has been variously translated. Weymouth has "sincere minds," the *NEB*, "honest thought," and the *TCNT*, "better feelings." The idea is that by his letters Peter wants to stir up or stimulate their capacity for morally sound spiritual judgment. He does this, according to the *NEB*, by "recalling to you what you already know." He is not bringing some novel idea or insight but calling them back to the basic truths they have always known. Wholesome thinking is thinking that proceeds from a pure mind. In Philippians 4

Paul emphasized the power of pure thought. Whatever things are true, noble, right, and pure should fill the mind of the Christian (Phil. 4:8).

2 Peter wants his readers *to recall the words spoken in the past by the holy prophets.* These would include not only the oracles of the Old Testament prophets but the utterances of their Christian counterparts as well. The New Testament prophets were men appointed by God to be his spokesmen to the early church. John the Baptist was a prophet (Luke 1:76), as were others in the early days of Christianity (see Acts 13:1; 1 Cor. 12:28; Eph. 3:5; etc.).

They are also to recall *the command given by our Lord and Savior through your apostles.* There is no immediate indication of exactly what Peter is referring to by the Lord's "command," but the context would suggest that it has to do with his expected return. Matthew 24 records Jesus' discourse on the end of the age. Such teaching would be a "command" in the sense that it counsels personal readiness for the great event and endurance in the trials that accompany its approach. "He who stands firm to the end will be saved" (Matt. 24:13). This information was constantly being taught to new believers by the apostles. The expression "your apostles" does not indicate that the author of 2 Peter could not have been one of the twelve apostles—although it is often cited as proof of that theory. The apostles are *your* apostles in the sense that they brought the message to *you.*

3 *First of all,* or, to begin with, *you must understand that in the last days scoffers will come.* The presence of those who mock God is itself an indication that the last days have come (1 Pet. 1:20 speaks of Christ having been revealed "in these last times"). The early church was convinced it was living in the twilight of history. While the Jews of the Old Testament looked forward to a coming age, the church declared that with the advent of Christ it had arrived. Before long Christ would return and a state of eternal blessedness would begin. This last step would be preceded by a time of distress and suffering. Scoffers were to be expected in this final period (see 1 Tim. 4:1-3 for another de-

scription of the same people). They will come *scoffing and
following their own evil desires.* Far from being led by the
Spirit of God, they are governed by their own passions. Note
that the mockers are within the church. This is not the taunting of those outside the congregation—unbelievers disinter-
ested in the Christian faith—but it comes from those who
profess to be followers of Christ. *They* are the ones denying
that he will return. By rejecting the doctrine of Christ's return they thought they had made a case for immoral conduct.
Why not sow your wild oats since the reaper will never return? In all of this they are following the evil inclinations of
their fallen natures.

4   The argument of the mockers can be reduced to the
principle that whatever has not yet happened never will.
*They will say, "Where is this 'coming' he promised? Ever
since our fathers died, everything goes on as it has since the
beginning of creation."* The way the question is put implies
that the promise is farfetched and without substance. Jeremiah's enemies kept saying, "Where is the word of the Lord?
Let it now be fulfilled!" (Jer. 17:15). The assumption was
that God doesn't speak. Likewise the assumption of the scoffers is that the Lord never did promise to return. Life continues as it always has. We live in a stable universe, and ever
since the world was created night follows day with perfect
regularity. Catastrophic events like those associated with the
supposed return of Christ simply do not happen in an ordered universe.

5-6   That is exactly where they are wrong, counters Peter. *They deliberately forget that long ago by God's word
the heavens existed and the earth was formed out of water
and with water. By water also the world of that time was
deluged and destroyed.* The universe is *not* stable. It has not
moved along without interruption since creation. In the time
of Noah God intervened and destroyed mankind in a great
flood. So much for the argument of a nonintervening God!

Unrelated to the mainstream of Peter's argument, but of
interest, is the cosmology (or view of the world) reflected in
the passage. It teaches that the earth was formed "out of

water." This translation seems to imply that water was the basic element from which the universe was made. The appropriate background, however, is Genesis 1:9, which teaches that God gathered the water to one place in order to "let dry ground appear." It is in this sense that the earth was formed "out of water." The *NTBE* has the earth being "lifted out of the water."

Slightly more difficult is the statement that the earth was formed "with water." *TCNT* has the earth being formed "by the action of water," that is, the water separated and the earth appeared. But that would say essentially the same as the previous phrase. Most commentators take the sentence to mean that the earth not only emerged out of water but that life on earth is sustained *by means of* water (i.e., rain).

As water was involved in the creation of the world, so it played the major role in the earth's destruction in the time of Noah. The *NIV* overrides a minor problem in verse 6 by translating "by water also." The Greek text has a plural relative pronoun that requires a double antecedent ("through which [things] the world at that time . . ."). The reference seems to be to the water and to the word of God (v. 5) acting as the agents both of creation and of destruction. God decreed and the waters carried out his will.

7 It is *by the same word* that *the present heavens and earth are reserved for fire.* God spoke and the earth came into being. God speaks again and the universe is reserved for fire. The Old Testament is replete with references to judgment by fire. "The Lord Almighty will come with . . . flames of a devouring fire" (Isa. 29:6). His arm will descend "with raging anger and consuming fire" (Isa. 30:30). The New Testament speaks of the revelation of Christ from heaven "in a blaze of fire" (Goodspeed) to take vengeance on the godless (2 Thess. 1:8). The first great universal judgment was by water; the last will be by fire. Some have suggested that the expression should read "stored up with fire" and find in it a precondition for nuclear explosion. While later verses (10 and 12) portray a scene that could be effected by nuclear holocaust, the Greek text of verse 7 does not require it. The

Stoics believed that fire was the prime element and that periodically the universe is destroyed by fire only to start its cycle over again. Nothing happens that hasn't happened before. But this doctrine of destruction by fire is far removed from what Peter is saying. The implications of the biblical doctrine of destruction by fire are ethical in intent. Since the universe will be destroyed by fire, God's people ought to live lives of holiness (see vv. 11, 18).

The present universe is *being kept for the day of judgment and destruction of ungodly men.* God is a moral being and will not let wickedness go unpunished. A day of judgment awaits the ungodly. Their end is destruction. As surely as God passed judgment in the time of Noah, he will once again repay the ungodly for their wickedness.

8 Not only are the scoffers wrong in their view that God will not intervene in history, but they are also wrong in assuming that he has to act according to their human timetable. *But do not forget this one thing, dear friends: With the Lord a day is like a thousand years, and a thousand years are like a day.* He is under no compulsion to carry out his promise according to man's understanding of time. In eternal matters time is quite irrelevant. The saying comes from Psalm 90:4, "For a thousand years in your sight are like a day that has just gone by." Peter is not conjuring up a mathematical equation that will explain why Christ has not yet returned. He is simply contrasting the eternity of God with the impatient expectations of man. Unfortunately, the verse has been pressed into the service of many who make mathematical predictions about the end of the age. Note, however, that not only are a thousand years like a day, but *a day is like a thousand years!* No reasonable calculations are possible.

9 *The Lord is not slow in keeping his promise, as some understand slowness.* The scoffers held that God must be negligent in carrying through on his promise. After all, look at how much time has passed and he has not yet returned. If not negligent, perhaps he is unable to fulfill his promise. The taunts remind us of Elijah's mocking of the priests of

Baal. "Perhaps [your god] is deep in thought, or busy, or traveling. Maybe he is sleeping " (1 Kings 18:28).

Not so, says Peter. God has not as yet returned to gather his own and bring punishment on the ungodly because *he is patient with you, not wanting anyone to perish, but everyone to come to repentance.* God is long-suffering. Although the wickedness of man calls for immediate action, God restrains his righteous anger and postpones judgment. The reason is simple: he does not want anyone to perish. Here is the true nature of God. He loves mankind and wants everyone to accept that love. Men perish because they are unwilling to let go of their sin. In the sacrifice of Jesus God did everything he could do for the salvation of man. The unconditional offer of eternal life is extended to all men, but each must freely accept. No one is lost because God has willed it. Paul writes to Timothy with crystal clarity, "God . . . wants all men to be saved and to come to a knowledge of the truth" (1 Tim. 2:4).

It is God's desire that everyone should come to repentance. To the contemptuous Paul puts the question, Do you not realize that God's kindness, tolerance, and patience are intended to lead you toward repentance? (Rom. 2:4). God does not coerce. He draws men. If they do not respond to his kindness they are beyond help. When righteous retribution comes, it will be too late to repent. Condemnation is the result of man's refusal to accept God's provision for life. "God did not send his Son into the world to condemn the world, but to save the world through him" (John 3:17).

10 God in his forebearance has postponed the day of his return in order that men may have as much time as possible to repent and believe. No one is to conclude, however, that he has changed his mind about the basic issues. *The day of the Lord will come.* In the Old Testament the day of the Lord was pictured as a time of victory for Israel (Joel 3:14-18) but a time of darkness and defeat for her enemies (Isa. 13:9-11). Peter describes the return of Christ in terms of the day of the Lord. It will bring relief to the troubled but punishment to the disobedient (2 Thess. 1:7-8). This day will come *like a thief*, suddenly, without warning (see 1 Thess. 5:2; also Rev. 3:3; 16:15). When men least expect it, suddenly he will return and the day of opportunity will be past.

The day of the Lord will be ushered in with an enormous cataclysm of fire. *The heavens will disappear with a roar; the elements will be destroyed by fire, and the earth and everything in it will be laid bare.* An awesome spectacle! Man marvels at the power of a single active volcano that can blow several cubic miles from the top of a mountain, pour molten lava over the surrounding landscape, and send its debris around the world in the upper atmosphere. What will it be like when the entire universe explodes into a fiery furnace! (See Mark 13:24-25 and Rev. 6:12-14 for further references to the final cosmic cataclysm.) The elements that will "melt with fervent heat" (the *AV* is better here; *NEB* has "disintegrate in flames") are probably the heavenly bodies—the stars, sun, moon, and planets, although the earth itself may also be in view. The verb in the final clause of verse 10 is obscure. Its basic meaning in the passive voice is "to be found." Thus some have suggested that the final clause may be a rhetorical question—that is, Will the earth and everything in it even be found? The answer, of course, would be, No!

Many have suggested that verse 10 (along with v. 12) predicts the end of our physical universe by a series of nuclear explosions. Dr. Earl Radmacher, President of Western Baptist Theological Seminary, recently reported that "on March 5, 1979, nine U.S. satellites simultaneously radioed back to earth that a gamma radiation explosion occurred in a nearby galaxy known as N-49. This explosion lasted for only one-tenth of a second, but released more radiation than our sun does in 3,000 years. Doyle Evans, an astrophysicist at the Los Alamos Scientific Laboratories in New Mexico, noted that had this explosion of energy occurred in our galaxy, it would have *instantly vaporized the earth!*" Whether or not this will be the specific way God achieves final judgment is not known. What is certain, however, is that as God once brought upon the world a judgment by water, so in the last days he will bring about a judgment by fire.

BEYOND THE FINAL HOLOCAUST (3:11-18)

11 Barclay writes that Peter is primarily interested in "the moral dynamics of the second coming." Certainly the ethical implications of universal destruction by fire are perfectly clear. *Since everything will be destroyed in this way*, Peter asks the obvious and crucial question, *What kind of people ought you to be?* If everything is about to go up in flames (is "on the verge of dissolution" is the way Weymouth handles the present participle), what does this imply about the way Christian people ought to conduct themselves. If, as Paul has it, "what is seen is temporal" and "what is unseen is eternal" (2 Cor. 4:18), where we invest our time and energies is of crucial importance. Frantic attempts to mount the ladder of material success amount to nothing more than scurrying to get the best deck chair on a sinking ship.

Peter answers his own question—*You ought to live holy and godly lives*. In his first letter he wrote, "Just as he who called you is holy, so be holy in all you do" (1 Pet. 1:15). Now he reemphasizes the obligation of God's people to develop a family likeness to God the Father. The word translated "godly" means a devout and reverent attitude that is pleasing to God.

12a Holy living should take place with an eye to the future. Believers are to live godly lives as they *look forward to the day of God*. An air of expectancy runs throughout the New Testament. The last recorded statement of Jesus is, "Yes, I am coming soon" (Rev. 22:20). Many of his parables counseled watchfulness (the ten virgins, Matt. 25:1-13; the talents, Matt. 25:14-30). Although 2,000 years have passed and his return is still future, the need for prayerful expectancy is still critical. It reminds us of the transient nature of this life and helps us to fix our attention on that which is eternal. The "day of God" is more than simply the return of Christ. It includes the entire sequence of events that brings this age to a close and ushers in the eternal state. It involves the vindication of the righteous, the punishment of the wicked, and the complete and final establishment of the eternal reign of God.

Not only do we look forward to the day of God, but we are able to *speed its coming*. Jesus taught us to pray, "Thy Kingdom, let it come" (Matt. 6:10). He also taught that before the end would come his gospel would be preached to the whole world (Matt. 24:14). So by prayer and preaching we hasten the coming of the day of God. And there is yet a third way. In the Talmud (the official collection of Jewish tradition and interpretation) there is a well-known saying that if Israel would repent for a single day the Messiah would appear. Peter would agree that by obedient and holy lives the church actually speeds the coming of the day of divine reckoning.

12b-13 Although *that day will bring about the destruction of the heavens by fire, and the elements will melt in the heat* (see v. 10 for comments), as Christians we are able to look beyond and *in keeping with his promise we are looking forward to a new heaven and a new earth.* The universe we now know will be destroyed with fire, but something new will take its place. Through Isaiah the prophet God promised to create "new heavens and a new earth" (Isa. 65:17). In his vision of the eternal state John saw "a new heaven and a new earth, for the first heaven and the first earth had passed away" (Rev. 21:1). The distinctive thing about this new order is that it will be *the home of righteousness*. The old order was dominated by sin. The new order will be permeated with righteousness.

14 People who anticipate an age of perfect righteousness are bound to live differently now. Peter writes, *So then, dear friends, since you are looking forward to this, make every effort to be found spotless, blameless and at peace with him.* Work at it. Make it your major concern. The verb ("make every effort") is a favorite of Peter (see 2 Pet. 1:10, 15; see also the noun form in 1:5). It reflects the zeal and enthusiasm of the man himself. Nothing halfhearted will do. The false teachers are blots (*spiloi*) and blemishes (*mōmoi*)

(2 Pet. 2:13). God's children are to be spotless (*aspiloi*) and blameless (*amōmētoi*)—the exact opposite of those who would destroy the faith and undermine the conduct of the church.

To be at peace with God means to live in fellowship with him. It begins with reconciliation, but it continues with daily confession of sin and openness to all God wants to do in the human heart. Theologically the believer *has peace* with God. The enmity caused by sin has been removed. Not always, however, does he enjoy the closeness of fellowship that was made available by Christ's death upon the cross. The accumulation of daily sin obscures the fact that Christ is near. Shortly before his death Jesus told Peter, "A person who has had a bath [regeneration] needs only to wash his feet [daily cleansing]" (John 13:10). Seek diligently to be found "at peace with him."

15 *Bear in mind that our Lord's patience means salvation.* The "delay" in his return is due to his concern that everyone might have every possible chance to come to him for salvation. He is the loving Father who each evening waits at the door of salvation and longs for the return of the prodigal. Regard his long-suffering as part of his saving plan. The door will remain open until the last possible moment.

Peter is not alone in his emphasis upon living blameless lives in view of the approaching return of Christ. He adds, *just as our dear brother Paul also wrote you.* Scholars enjoy debating which letter by Paul it was that Peter had in mind. Galatians? Ephesians? Colossians? Probably Peter referred to no specific letter but to Paul's general theme of holy living in view of the imminent return of Christ. Berkeley has, "in all the letters in which he mentions these subjects." Note the affection that Peter has for his fellow apostle. He is "our dear brother." Although Peter was the apostle to the Jews and Paul the apostle to the Gentiles (Gal. 2:8), and although Paul had to correct Peter publicly at Antioch (Gal. 2:11-16), there existed between these two early leaders of the church a deep appreciation and a bond of brotherly love. Peter freely acknowledges that Paul wrote to them *with the wisdom that*

God gave him. No one apostle has a corner on divine revelation or wisdom. God distributes his gifts through chosen
men, and Paul, although not one of the favored Twelve, is
nevertheless a genuine apostle and spokesman for God.

16 Peter was not the first nor was he the last who upon
reading Paul has been led to confess that *His letters contain
some things that are hard to understand.* In the larger context of 2 Peter these difficult or ambiguous things refer to the
return of Christ. That was the basic doctrine the heretics
were denying. The word translated "hard to understand"
was commonly used in secular Greek in connection with the
oracles of the gods. Almost by definition these utterances
were obscure and ambiguous.

These difficult portions by Paul are said to be *distort[ed]*
by *ignorant and unstable people.* Again Peter is taking the
false teachers to task. Phillips calls them "ill informed and
unbalanced." Their understanding of the issues is limited
and their unsteady character leads them quickly into error.
The word *distort* originally meant the tightening of a cable
with a windlass. The figure came quite naturally to be applied to the straining and twisting of the meaning of words.
Not only do the troublemakers distort what Paul has written,
but they handle other sacred texts in the same way. Peter
writes, *as they do the other Scriptures.* This statement gives
an important insight into how the early church viewed the
writings of Paul and other apostles. Paul's letters are placed
on a par with "the other Scriptures." What he had to say was
accepted as the word of God. In perhaps the first letter Paul
ever wrote to a believing congregation he thanked God that
the message he preached was accepted "not as the word of
men, but as it actually is, the word of God" (1 Thess. 2:13).
His letters were equally the mind of God. They were *Scripture.* Those who tamper with God's Word do it *to their own
destruction.* God's Word is not an idle philosophical toy but
the dynamic presence of God himself expressed through the
lips of an inspired author (see 1 Pet. 1:20-21).

17 *Therefore, dear friends* (note the frequency of this
expression—four times in Chapter 3: vv. 1, 8, 14, 17), *since*

you already know this (you are forewarned by this letter),
*be on your guard so that you may not be carried away by
the error of lawless men and fall from your secure position.*
Error is not the cause of lawlessness; it is the result. Heresy
begins by a decision to change the way one lives. Once the
decision has been made to disobey, human nature searches
out some basis to support its willful acts. At this point truth
is twisted and pressed into service for a deviant lifestyle.
Men go wrong not because some sort of evidence forces
them in a particular direction but because they need to ra-
tionalize a prior decision to disobey.

The *NIV*'s "secure position" sounds as if the Christians
were in danger of falling from a secure faith into error. The
strong foundation was that laid by the apostles and prophets.
This foundation was secure, but their footing upon it was
less than stable. Newly won to Christ (2 Pet. 2:18), many
were not as yet grounded in the essential truths of the faith.
These are the ones especially susceptible to the deceitful
practices of the false teachers.

18 The answer to error is to grow in one's Christian
faith. So Peter concludes his letter, *But grow in the grace
and knowledge of our Lord and Savior Jesus Christ.* Let
your experience in Christ continue to mature. May his gracious favor become increasingly apparent in all that you say
and do. Learn to know him personally in an ever increasing
way. He is Lord and Savior. He redeems and rules. And he
is *our* Lord.

The benediction is simple: *To him be glory both now
and forever! Amen.* The object of devotion is Christ. May
his name be praised now and throughout eternity. Amen,
may it ever be true.

QUESTIONS FOR DISCUSSION

FIRST PETER ONE

1. What does it mean to be an apostle?
2. What is said in verse 2 about each member of the trinity?
3. To what extent should Christian sojourners settle down in this world?
4. Explain each name in the title "Lord Jesus Christ."
5. Why do you think conversion is called a "new birth"?
6. What great event makes the Christian hope a *living* hope?
7. We often think of salvation as something that took place in the past. What does verse 5 tell us about another tense of salvation?
8. Why do Christians have to suffer grief in all kinds of trials?
9. In what sense is Christian joy "inexpressible"?
10. Who were "the prophets" of verse 10? Did they live before or after Christ?
11. What were these prophets trying to figure out?
12. Why did popular Jewish sentiment refuse the idea of a suffering Messiah?
13. What did the prophets learn about the "time and circumstances" of which they spoke?
14. What is the fundamental reason why Christians are to be holy?

15. What does it mean to be holy? How would you interpret this requirement in view of the permissive social atmosphere of twentieth-century America?
16. Why is there no inconsistency between salvation by faith and judgment by works?
17. Believers in Peter's day were redeemed from an "empty way of life" handed down from their ancestors. Can this be said of life in contemporary America? In what way is life apart from Christ "empty"?
18. What does it mean that Christ was a sacrificial lamb?
19. How does obedience purify?

FIRST PETER TWO

1. Why is the word of God so important in the life of a Christian?
2. In what sense is Christ a *"living* stone"?
3. What are some of the "spiritual sacrifices" offered by the church?
4. Why do people stumble over the message of Christ?
5. What significance do you find in the fact that titles given to Israel in the Old Testament are transferred to the church in the New Testament?
6. What does it mean that the church is a "holy nation"? Would an outsider come to this conclusion watching how the average congregation lives? If not, what can we do about it?
7. Why would Peter be classed as an ethical realist?
8. In what sense are we (and to what extent should we be) "strangers in the world"?
9. What attitude is the Christian to take toward civil authority? Are there exceptions? Explain.
10. What higher authority is flouted when civil law is disobeyed?
11. Give an example of how good works have silenced an uninformed critic.
12. Explain how free men can live as servants of God.

13. Why was it appropriate for slaves to submit to masters even though they were harsh?
14. Why do you think Christians have been called to a life of unjust suffering?
15. Are twentieth-century Christians suffering? If not, why not?
16. On what basis was Jesus convinced that the Father would raise him from the dead?
17. What are some of the implications that flow from the fact that Christ died so that we might "die to sins" and "live for righteousness"?

FIRST PETER THREE

1. How does the first-century context of Peter's admonition that wives submit to their husbands affect how we apply that teaching in the twentieth century?
2. What is "silent evangelism"? Is it always better than the spoken word? Why/why not?
3. Is a Christian wife obligated to obey a non-Christian husband? Any exceptions?
4. In what sense are husbands and wives *heirs* with one another of the full blessing of life?
5. Why would a "non-loving Christian" be a contradiction of terms?
6. Christ humbled himself by going to the cross. How are we to humble ourselves?
7. In what sense is eternal life a present reality?
8. Why can prayerlessness be considered a personal insult to God?
9. What would happen in your local church if the members seriously became "zealots of the good"?
10. Can the Christian faith be defended rationally or is faith by definition a leap into the dark? Explain.
11. Give an example of how evil can be overcome with good.
12. What are the implications of the fact that Christ died "once for all"?

13. Who are the "spirits in prison" to whom Christ preached?
14. In what sense did Christ *preach* to the imprisoned spirits?
15. In what sense does baptism save?
16. What is implied by the fact that Jesus is at God's right hand?

FIRST PETER FOUR

1. Was Christ's suffering more than physical? Explain.
2. What is the theological basis for the Christian giving up sin as a way of life?
3. Why do immoral people object to those who pursue what is moral?
4. In what sense is the "end of history" more than a point in time?
5. Two thousand years ago Peter said that the end was near. Since history is still going on, how do you explain Peter's statement?
6. What is the essence of Christian love?
7. Explain "love covers a multitude of sins."
8. In what sense does genuine preaching involve a miracle?
9. Why would Gentile Christians be more surprised than their Jewish friends when they met active opposition?
10. Why doesn't the contemporary American church meet with opposition from the world?
11. In what sense do believers share in the suffering of Christ?
12. What is meant by "preparatory judgment"?
13. What is meant by the statement that men do not decide on the truthfulness of the gospel?

FIRST PETER FIVE

1. Trace the history of the idea of eldership.

2. What is the primary responsibility of an elder?
3. What is implied by the statement that God is a gentleman?
4. Why does greed for money disqualify a person from serving as an elder?
5. What will be the ultimate reward for faithfulness?
6. Explain the difference between a revolution in the interests of disorder and a revolution against disorder. How does submission to authority relate to this?
7. Why must ethics have a theological base?
8. On what basis are we called upon to cast our anxieties on God?
9. What is intended by the imagery of Satan as a prowling lion?
10. How could Peter, an unlearned fisherman, write such polished Greek as we find in 1 Peter?
11. What would a modern day "Silas" be like? What kind of activities would he be involved in in your church?
12. Who is "she who is in Babylon"?
13. What was the "kiss of love"?

SECOND PETER ONE

1. Would there be any serious implications if we were to deny that Peter the apostle wrote Second Peter?
2. How does the Judeo-Christian concept of "slave" differ from the Greco-Roman?
3. How do grace and peace come to the believer? Explain.
4. In what sense does the believer participate in the divine nature?
5. In what sense is godliness more than devotion to God?
6. How can believers make their election sure?
7. Explain the statement, "To be established in the truth means more than to understand what it says."
8. In what way is the death of a Christian an "Exodus"?

9. On what event does Peter argue the return of Christ? How does this differ from other New Testament writers?
10. What does it mean to speak anthropomorphically of God?
11. What implications may be drawn from the fact that Christ is the "morning star"?
12. What is the role of the Holy Spirit in prophetic teaching?

SECOND PETER TWO

1. What was it in the Old Testament setting that made a false prophet *false?*
2. List and explain two different ways of denying Christ.
3. Why does heretical teaching attract so many followers?
4. Give one example of how language is used to promote error rather than truth.
5. In what way did the angels sin? Which of the two interpretations is more satisfactory to you, and why?
6. On what basis can Lot be called a "righteous man"?
7. To what extent should Christians be distressed by the immorality of contemporary society?
8. Are the unrighteous dead being punished at the present time?
9. Why cannot people get along when everyone does what comes naturally?
10. On what basis does Peter compare false prophets with brute beasts?
11. What is the way of Balaam?
12. Why is the person who has thrown off all external restraint not free?
13. Why is it better not to know the truth than to know it and disobey?

SECOND PETER THREE

1. Is there any significance for us today in the fact that the scoffers spoken of by Peter were *inside* the church?
2. In what sense is the world formed "out of water"?
3. How will the second great universal judgment be carried out? Could this be a nuclear holocaust?
4. Why has God delayed bringing punishment on the ungodly?
5. Does God condemn or is condemnation the result of something else?
6. How will the day of the Lord come?
7. On what basis, according to Peter, are believers to live godly lives?
8. How can the church speed the coming of the day of the Lord?
9. How do false leaders "distort" the Scriptures? Can you think of any current examples?
10. Explain the statement, "Error is not the cause of lawlessness; it is the result."

INDEX OF SUBJECTS